The Extent of Restrictions on the Service of Active-Component Military Women

Laura L. Miller, Jennifer Kavanagh, Maria C. Lytell,
Keith Jennings, Craig Martin

Prepared for the Office of the Secretary of Defense
Approved for public release; distribution unlimited

RAND NATIONAL DEFENSE RESEARCH INSTITUTE

The research described in this report was prepared for the Office of the Secretary of Defense (OSD). The research was conducted within the RAND National Defense Research Institute, a federally funded research and development center sponsored by OSD, the Joint Staff, the Unified Combatant Commands, the Navy, the Marine Corps, the defense agencies, and the defense Intelligence Community under Contract W74V8H-06-C-0002.

Library of Congress Cataloging-in-Publication Data is available for this publication.

ISBN: 978-0-8330-5969-7

Cover: Female Engagement Team members Pfc. Kelly Shutka, Pfc. Rachel Miller, and Sgt. Richelle Aus patrol a bazaar in Zabul province, Afghanistan. Photo by Seth Robson. Copyright Stars and Stripes. Used with permission.

Published 2012 by the RAND Corporation
1776 Main Street, P.O. Box 2138, Santa Monica, CA 90407-2138
1200 South Hayes Street, Arlington, VA 22202-5050
4570 Fifth Avenue, Suite 600, Pittsburgh, PA 15213-2665
RAND URL: http://www.rand.org/
To order RAND documents or to obtain additional information, contact
Distribution Services: Telephone: (310) 451-7002;
Fax: (310) 451-6915; Email: order@rand.org

Preface

Despite a historical increase in the number and types of positions open to women in the U.S. military, gender restrictions continue to affect the types of positions they can fill. Recent reports have questioned the validity of military exclusion policies and called for their repeal. For example, the 2011 final report of the Military Leadership Diversity Commission stated that U.S. Department of Defense (DoD) and military service exclusionary policies regarding the assignment of women are institutional barriers to women's career advancement and to greater gender diversity among senior military leaders. The commission recommended eliminating these policies. The U.S. Congress, through the 2011 National Defense Authorization Act, required the Secretary of Defense, in coordination with the secretaries of the military departments, to review gender-restrictive laws, policies, and regulations to determine whether changes are needed to ensure that female personnel have equitable opportunities to compete and excel in the armed forces. To accomplish this assessment, the Under Secretary of Defense for Personnel and Readiness initiated the Women in the Services Review (WISR), comprising a senior leader steering committee and a working group with representatives from the Air Force, Army, Marine Corps, and Navy.

In support of the WISR, the Under Secretary of Defense for Personnel and Readiness asked the RAND Corporation to document military occupations that were closed to female service members as of 2011, as well as occupations that were open to women but with some positions that were closed. RAND was asked to pursue additional information for a few of the open occupations to determine the nature of the restrictions and to illuminate the potential career implications of assignment policies. The RAND researchers' effort included providing, where possible, the service justification for the closures and quantifying the extent of these restrictions in the active components for fiscal year 2011. For occupations in which some but not all positions were closed to women, the researchers provided additional information by reporting the percentage of active-component women serving in those occupations as of December 2010. For a limited number of occupations, the researchers explored the nature of the closures, possible implications for career progression, and additional details about the degree of closure and women's representation by pay grade. This report does not evaluate whether the current policies should be revised. However, it offers recommendations to the services about ways to improve its gender-restriction databases.

This research was sponsored by the Under Secretary of Defense for Personnel and Readiness and conducted within the Forces and Resources Policy Center of the RAND National Defense Research Institute, a federally funded research and development center sponsored by the Office of the Secretary of Defense, the Joint Staff, the Unified Combatant Commands, the Navy, the Marine Corps, the defense agencies, and the defense Intelligence Community. For more information on the Forces and Resources Policy Center, see http://www.rand.org/nsrd/ndri/centers/frp.html or contact the director (contact information is provided on the web page). Comments or questions should be addressed to the project leader, Laura Miller, at Laura_Miller@rand.org, 703-413-1100 x5912.

Contents

Tables

Summary

Background

Women have long served in the U.S. military, although always as a minority. During wartime, women's level of participation has expanded to meet the demand for military personnel; this was particularly true during World War II (Godson, 2002; Holm, 1993; Moore, 1996; Poulos, 1996; Segal, 1995). In the 1970s, an unprecedented increase in women's participation in the civilian labor force, coupled with the advent of the all-volunteer force in 1973, changed the thinking of the U.S. Department of Defense (DoD) and the military services with regard to the roles women could play in the armed forces. The services could no longer simply draft the number of individuals needed; they had to recruit them. To help fill their ranks, the services opened more roles to women, but within a set of rules designed to protect women from the possibility of being captured, injured, or killed by the enemy and to preserve privacy in living conditions.

For the Army and Marine Corps, initial thoughts about where women could be assigned were shaped by the perception of a linear battlefield, with a dangerous "front" and a comparatively safer "rear," with certain units (e.g., combat arms battalions and below in the Army) designed to directly combat an enemy on the ground and other units (e.g., service support units, command units) designed to serve behind those units and not directly confront the enemy. Women could be assigned jobs in the units expected to be located in the rear but not those expected to serve at the front. In 1988, the system was formalized when DoD promulgated the "risk rule," which banned women from units or occupations in which the risk of exposure to direct combat or capture was equal to or greater than that of combat units in the same theater.

However, during the Gulf War of 1991, women were among the military personnel who participated in combat flying operations, served within range of enemy artillery, served with ground combat units and in some cases ahead of other combat units, were exposed to enemy hostilities, and received service combat awards. As a result, in 1994, the risk rule was jettisoned and replaced by one that said women could be assigned to any position for which they were qualified, except in units whose primary purpose was direct ground combat. The new policy also contained criteria under which the services could, but were not required to, retain gender restrictions:

> where the Service Secretary attests that the costs of appropriate berthing or privacy arrangements are prohibitive;
>
> where units and positions are doctrinally required to physically collocate and remain with direct ground combat units that are closed to women;
>
> where units are engaged in long range reconnaissance operations and Special Operations Forces missions; and
>
> where job related physical requirements would necessarily exclude the vast majority of women Service members. (Aspin, 1994)

Under this policy today, women's representation in the services ranges from a low of 7 percent in the Marine Corps to a high of 19 percent in the Air Force.

Although opportunities for women have expanded substantially in all services, the Military Leadership Diversity Commission noted that women were underrepresented in both the senior noncommissioned officer and flag and general officer ranks and that they had significantly lower retention rates. The commission cited combat exclusion policies as an important barrier for female service members and recommended that the services eliminate all combat exclusion policies for women. The 2011 National Defense Authorization Act directed the Secretary of Defense and the service secretaries to review all policies and regulations to determine whether they needed to be changed to ensure that female service members have equitable opportunities to serve.

Purpose

In response, the Under Secretary of Defense for Personnel and Readiness established the Women in the Services Review (WISR) to review all restrictive policies, regulations, and laws to determine whether they prevent women from competing and excelling in the U.S. armed forces. DoD asked RAND to support WISR's efforts by describing and quantifying the positions closed to women, pursuing additional information about perceived career implications for a few of the open occupations, and participating in WISR meetings. This report describes the current restrictions of women's service, relying primarily on policy and service authorization data, as well as service personnel data and communication with service representatives. RAND researchers focused on describing occupations that are entirely closed to women as well as occupations that are open to them but with positions in some units closed. For a limited number of open occupations, additional details about the extent of the restrictions and potential implications of those restrictions are explored. This report does not debate the merits of the current policies.

Findings

The overwhelming majority of positions whose primary orientation is engaging the enemy with deadly force from the ground are in the Army and the Marine Corps. Gender restrictions based on direct ground combat close off to women entire occupations in the combat arms, as well as some types of units entirely, regardless of the occupations they include. In units not engaged in combat, some positions are also closed because of the requirement that the incumbent come from occupations closed to women or hold additional skills that women cannot obtain under current policies.

Special operations occupations closed to women are physically demanding—even for men who attempt to enter them. The elite status of the special forces means that some of the most prestigious military occupations are closed to women. However, not all positions in special operations commands are closed to women.

DoD policy gives the services the discretion to close positions to women that would require collocation with direct ground combat units. The way the forces operate today, frequent interaction of support personnel and units with direct ground combat units is common and necessary. Women have been serving successfully in non–direct ground combat missions in Iraq and Afghanistan at the same camps and forward operating bases as direct ground combat units but without being assigned to those units. They have traveled on dangerous roads in convoys and intermingled with local populations. The Secretary of the Army reported that more than 13,000 positions in the Army are closed to women due solely to the collocation restriction.

In the Navy, many restrictions are due to berthing and privacy limitations, because of the expense of modifying seagoing vessels, and generally apply to enlisted women, because officers on ships enjoy a higher degree of privacy. Most Navy specialties that are closed to women due to berthing and privacy constraints are submarine specialties. However, the first female officers trained to serve on submarines graduated in the fall of 2011. To provide privacy for enlisted men and women on submarines, modifications of existing berthing configurations will be necessary.

To provide greater flexibility in meeting the Navy's needs, and to better sustain women's opportunities for sea-duty assignments, the revised Navy policy requires future ship modifications to provide gender-neutral modular designs.

Recommendations for Improved Recordkeeping

Over the course of this research effort, we discovered instances of ambiguity, errors, and conflicting information about whether positions were closed to women. Thus, we recommend that the services improve the tracking, accuracy, and visibility of positions closed to military women.

All positions that are closed to women should be coded to reflect all applicable closures. This would provide visibility to DoD and service leadership about what is closed and also help detailers, career field managers, and requesting and receiving commanders consistently apply exclusion policies, which, in some cases, are open to differing interpretations and have been inconsistently applied.

Acknowledgments

We begin by thanking Lernes J. Hebert, Director of Officer and Enlisted Personnel Management, a component of the Office of the Deputy Assistant Secretary of Defense for Military Personnel Policy, who provided oversight and guidance for this effort. We are also indebted to members of his staff, particularly our project monitors, Carl "Doug" Johnson and Air Force Lieutenant Colonel Mark T. Horner. Both routinely provided transparency on the development of WISR goals and progress and greatly facilitated coordination with the services to provide access to the data needed for these analyses.

This report would not have been possible without the contributions of service representatives to the WISR working group, who facilitated access to databases, provided information about service policies and practices, coordinated input from other service representatives (such as community and career field managers), and verified report content. From the Air Force, we would like to thank Lieutenant Colonel Jennifer Allee, Lieutenant Colonel Donna Pike, Major Lamont A. Coleman, and Major Kevin R. Jernigan. From the Army, we appreciate the assistance of Colonel David Griffith, Colonel Edward J. Seigfried, and Major Trina Rice. From the Marine Corps, we thank Colonel John G. Nettles, Lieutenant Colonel William J. McWaters, Major Ian C. Fletcher, Major Paul J. Hilliard, Major Arturo Manzanedo, and Captain Ronald A. Garrick. From the Navy, the service whose data were most challenging to code and characterize, we thank Lieutenant Commander Jean Marie Sullivan, Lieutenant Maura C. Garrity, and John Acker for their extensive efforts to provide the data and additional Navy points of contact we needed.

An earlier draft of this manuscript was reviewed by Mady W. Segal, professor emerita at the University of Maryland, College Park, and Lawrence Hanser at RAND. They conducted thorough peer reviews within a very short time frame, and we appreciate their dedication to the effort. Beth Asch, associate director of the Forces and Resources Policy Institute in the RAND National Defense Research Institute, oversaw the quality-assurance process and provided valuable feedback on an earlier draft as well.

Also at RAND, we acknowledge the early project conceptualization and leadership of Margaret C. Harrell, now a senior fellow and director of the Joining Forces Initiative at the Center for a New American Security. We also benefited from the wisdom of our colleague Bernard Rostker, who has experience and expertise in managing military personnel issues and provided detailed comments on a prior draft. Harry Thie's insights regarding manpower authorization and personnel data also aided our research. John E. Boon provided research assistance, Hosay Salam and Anny Wong assisted with content and formatting of some of the data tables, and James McGee helped prepare the berthing limitations table in Appendix D. Perry Firoz, Laurie McDonald, Rodger Madison, Judith Mele, and Carra Sims assisted with data acquisition and formatting. Jerry Sollinger made valuable recommendations that improved the layout and readability of some of the tables and also helped draft the summary. Lauren Skrabala's expert editing elevated our writing, and she patiently worked with us through multiple drafts.

Abbreviations

AFSC	Air Force Specialty Code
ALO	air liaison officer
CBRN	chemical, biological, radiological, and nuclear
CWO	chief warrant officer
DACOWITS	Defense Advisory Committee on Women in the Services
DCPC	Direct Combat Probability Coding (Army)
DEERS PITE	Defense Enrollment Eligibility Reporting System Point in Time Extracts
DoD	U.S. Department of Defense
EMOS	exception military occupational specialty (Marine Corps)
FMOS	free military occupational specialty (Marine Corps)
HIMARS	High Mobility Artillery Rocket System
LDO	limited-duty officer (Marine Corps, Navy)
MLDC	Military Leadership Diversity Commission
MLRS	Multiple Launch Rocket System
MOS	military occupational specialty (Army, Marine Corps)
MPW	Authorized Manpower Master (Air Force)
NCO	noncommissioned officer
NEC	Navy Enlisted Classification
NGLO	naval gunfire liaison officer

OEF	Operation Enduring Freedom (Afghanistan)
OIF	Operation Iraqi Freedom
PMAD	Personnel Management Authorization Document (Army)
PMOS	primary military occupational specialty (Marine Corps)
SEAL	sea-air-land (Navy)
TFMMS	Total Force Manpower Management System (Navy)
TFSMS	Total Force Structure Management System (Marine Corps)
WISR	Women in the Services Review

CHAPTER ONE

Introduction

Background

Women have long served in the U.S. military, although always as a minority.[1] During wartime, women's level of participation has expanded to meet the demand for military personnel; this was particularly true during World War II (Godson, 2002; Holm, 1993; Moore, 1996; Poulos, 1996; Segal, 1995). The question of how women should be integrated into the U.S. military and, specifically, the role they should play in combat operations became particularly salient with the advent of the all-volunteer force in 1973. An unprecedented increase in women's participation in the civilian labor force, the expected ratification of the Equal Rights Amendment, and the end of the draft in 1973 changed the thinking of the U.S. Department of Defense (DoD) and the military services with regard to the roles women could play in the armed forces (Holm, 1993). The services could no longer simply draft the number of personnel they needed; they had to recruit them. To help fill the ranks, the services opened more roles and pursued the goal of increasing the representation of women in the armed forces (Rostker, 2006).

Additionally, external forces expanded assignment opportunities for women, such as a 1975 congressional mandate that women be allowed admission to the military service academies and judicial and congressional actions that opened up service on noncombatant ships to Navy women in 1978 (Holm, 1993). Subsequent studies and debates over the proper assignment of military women have involved the U.S. Congress, the DoD, the services, academic scholars, and appointed task forces and commissions. However, the question of how women should serve continued to raise a number of complex—and contentious—issues.[2]

---

1 For a detailed history of women's roles in the U.S. military through the Gulf War, see Holm, 1993.

2 Controversies surrounding gender integration in the U.S. military are discussed in Binkin, 1993; Godson, 2002; Harrell and Miller, 1997; Holm, 1993; Iskra, 2007; Mitchell, 1998; Moore, 1996; Moskos, 1990; Presidential Commission on the Assignment of Women in the Armed Forces, 1992; Putko and Johnson, 2008; Rogan, 1981; Schneider and Schneider, 1992; Segal, 1995; Simon, 2001; Skaine, 1999; and Stiehm, 1981, 1989.

For the Army and Marine Corps, the initial thoughts on an expanded role for women were shaped by the perception of a linear battlefield, with a dangerous "front" and a comparatively safer "rear," with certain units (e.g., combat arms battalions and below in the Army) designed to directly combat an enemy on the ground and other units (e.g., service support units, command units) designed to serve behind those units and not directly confront the enemy. Women could be assigned jobs in the units intended to be located in the rear, but not those intended to serve at the front. In 1988, the system was formalized when DoD promulgated the "risk rule," which banned women from units or occupations in which the risk of exposure to direct combat or capture was equal to or greater than that of combat units in the same theater.

From the Gulf War to the Current Policy

The current DoD assignment policy emerged in the aftermath of the 1991 Gulf War. Nearly 41,000 American military women served in that theater of operations, and military commanders subsequently lauded their contributions (Holm, 1993, p. xiii). Secretary of Defense Dick Cheney asserted, "We could not have won without them" (Holm, 1993, p. xiv). Their roles included being stationed within enemy artillery range, moving into Iraq during the ground war, being nearby or attached to the rear of combat maneuver battalions as they moved across the battlefield, being geographically located ahead of some combat units, and earning combat flying time credit and Combat Medical Patches (Army) and Combat Action Ribbons (Marine Corps) (GAO, 1993, p. 20).

In April 1993, Congress repealed the 1948 law that prohibited women from being assigned to aircraft engaged in combat missions (which had been amended to permit exceptions for medical and legal personnel and chaplains). In November 1993, Congress repealed the naval combatant exclusion law that prohibited women from being permanently assigned to combatant ships. At the same time, it also prohibited DoD from opening additional combat positions to women without congressional review. Following those congressional actions, DoD opened up positions on combat helicopters and bomber and fighter aircraft to women. It also permitted women to be permanently assigned to surface combatant vessels, such as destroyers and aircraft carriers (Ebbert and Hall, 1999). In 1994, DoD rescinded its 1988 "risk rule," which had permitted bans on women in units or occupations with risk of exposure to direct combat, hostile fire, or capture that was equal to or greater than that of combat units in the same theater of operations (Holm, 1993; Rostker, 2006). The expanded role of military women during the 1991 Gulf War and the availability of long-range weapons revealed that everyone in theater was potentially at risk, rendering a risk-based policy impractical (GAO, 1993; Holm, 1993).

In 1994 then–Secretary of Defense Les Aspin rescinded the risk rule and established a new policy on the assignment of women, which remains in effect today. In the 1994 policy Aspin instructed,

> Service members are eligible to be assigned to all positions for which they are qualified, except that women shall be excluded from assignment to units below the brigade level whose primary mission is to engage in direct combat on the ground. (Aspin, 1994)

Women were no longer prohibited from serving in occupations or units with a primary mission of engaging in direct combat by air or sea. The policy memo defined direct ground combat as

> engaging an enemy on the ground with individual or crew served weapons while being exposed to hostile fire and to a high probability of direct physical contact with the hostile force's personnel. Direct ground combat takes place well forward on the battlefield while locating and closing with the enemy to defeat them by fire, maneuver, or shock effect. (Aspin, 1994)

Secretary Aspin also specified that the new policy should be used only to expand opportunities for women, not to close occupations or units that were already open. The Army's definition of direct ground combat predated the DoD definition and was not revised or discarded afterward. For the Army, direct combat is defined as

> [e]ngaging an enemy with individual or crew served weapons while being exposed to direct enemy fire, a high probability of direct physical contact with the enemy's personnel and a substantial risk of capture. Direct combat takes place while closing with the enemy by fire, maneuver, and shock effect in order to destroy or capture the enemy, or while repelling the enemy's assault by fire, close combat, or counterattack. (Army Regulation 600-13, 1992, p. 5)

The difference in definitions is significant because, among other issues, the Army's version still includes references to substantial risk of capture and repelling an enemy assault, which have implications for policy implementation (Harrell, Castaneda, et al., 2007).

In addition to requiring the services to ban women from direct ground combat, i.e., the "direct combat exclusion," Aspin's 1994 policy memo identified a set of criteria under which the services could choose, but were not required, to maintain gender restrictions:

> where the Service Secretary attests that the costs of appropriate *berthing or privacy arrangements* are prohibitive;

> where units and positions are doctrinally required to physically *collocate* and remain with direct ground combat units that are closed to women;
>
> where units are engaged in *long range reconnaissance operations and Special Operations Forces missions*; and
>
> where job related *physical requirements* would necessarily exclude the vast majority of women Service members. (Aspin, 1994; emphasis added)

The services were also permitted to propose additional exclusions, with justification to DoD.

As part of the implementation of the 1994 policy, each service was required to explicitly identify all units and positions within units that would open as a result of the elimination of the risk rule and the new direct ground combat definition, all those that would remain closed, and the explicit rationale for all closures from the list included in Aspin's memo. Overall, these legal and policy changes initially opened up more than 250,000 positions to women, with the largest impact in the Navy (in which the positions open to women increased from 61 percent to 91 percent, though without the berthing to fully accommodate them) and the Marine Corps (from 33 percent to 62 percent) (Harrell and Miller, 1997, p. 12). In the Navy, shore-only occupations were largely eliminated: Sea duty became an expectation for women as it had previously been for men (Harrell and Miller, 1997, p. 22).

As permitted under the 1994 policy, the services have continued to open to military women additional positions without direct ground combat as a primary mission.[3] For example, in 2010, the Marine Corps opened the officer and the enlisted counterintelligence/human intelligence occupations. In 2010, the Navy opened officer positions on ballistic and guided missile submarines to women.

It is important to note that the 1994 policy does not prohibit military women from *ever* serving in direct ground combat. By necessity, women can and do participate in direct ground combat. The restriction specifies that direct ground combat cannot be the *primary* mission of the units below the brigade level to which women are assigned.

Military Women's Expanding Roles in Iraq and Afghanistan

Military women have been increasingly integrated into U.S. military operations in Iraq and Afghanistan to meet the needs of the services. Prior to the current conflicts, in October 1998, the U.S. General Accounting Office (now the U.S. Government Accountability Office) reported,

---

[3] Title 10, Section 652, of the U.S. Code requires the Secretary of Defense to report to Congress any changes in its gender-exclusion policies.

> Ground combat experts in the Army and the Marine Corps note that, in the post–Cold War era, the nonlinear battlefield is becoming more common. Should this trend continue, defining direct ground combat as occurring "well forward on the battlefield" may become increasingly less descriptive of actual battlefield conditions. (GAO, 1998b, p. 10)

Like the mission environment in the 1990s in places such as Somalia, Haiti, and Bosnia, the battlefields in Iraq and Afghanistan are not linear. There is no line dividing the battlefield, with a highly dangerous "front," where all-male combat elements engage the enemy, and a relatively safe "rear" area containing the gender-integrated support elements. Military camps and operating bases have been surrounded by hostile territory and subjected to mortar attacks, rocket attacks, suicide bombers, and other types of enemy fire. Female personnel who travel or operate in convoys have suffered from improvised explosive devices hidden on roads, a key enemy tactic for killing or injuring U.S. military and contract personnel. Indeed, military women have earned combat distinctions. In 2005, Sergeant Leigh Ann Hester of the Kentucky Army National Guard's 617th Military Police Company became the first woman since World War II to be awarded a Silver Star, and the first woman ever to be awarded one for direct combat actions against an enemy (Soucy, 2008). In 2007, Army Specialist Monica Brown earned a Silver Star for her heroic actions in Afghanistan as a medic with the 782nd Brigade Support Battalion, 4th Brigade Combat Team, 82nd Airborne Division (Clare, 2008).

Navy representatives report that, in 2007, the Navy began temporarily assigning women to deploy with special warfare units that were not expecting to engage in direct ground combat during their deployment. (Direct ground combat is only one type of special operations mission.) Since that time, 10 to 15 female Sailors serving in open legal, intelligence, administrative, construction, and information technology occupations have deployed to the U.S. Central Command region with each Naval special warfare squadron.

Local cultural sensitivities in Iraq and Afghanistan have led the services to employ female personnel in missions led by combat units. The ground forces have created teams of military women (called Lioness Teams, Female Engagement Teams, or Cultural Support Teams) to serve alongside all-male infantry and special operations units and engage with the female population in theaters of operations (Bumiller, 2010; *Lioness*, 2008; Robson, 2010; Strauss, 2008; Talton, 2009; "Two Members of Cultural Support Team Receive Combat Action Badges," 2011). Women's primary roles in these counterinsurgency operations have included searching local women, providing medical treatment to local women, intelligence support, humanitarian assistance, and civil-military operations, although, on occasion, these units were engaged by the enemy (Bumiller, 2010; *Lioness*, 2008; Robson, 2010; Strauss, 2008; Talton, 2009; "Two Members of Cultural Support Team Receive Combat Action Badges," 2011).

These teams were created to meet operational needs, not as a form of affirmative action for military women.

Women's expanded efforts in the nation's wars have not come without a cost. According to the Defense Manpower Data Center, as of October 2011, 110 U.S. military women have died and 623 have been physically wounded in Operation Iraqi Freedom (OIF), no women have died and 12 have been physically wounded in Operation New Dawn (as OIF became known on September 1, 2010), and 31 women have died and 172 have been physically wounded as a part of Operation Enduring Freedom (OEF) in Afghanistan (DMDC, 2011). Although women have engaged the enemy and sustained injuries in these wars, this is not to say that they have served in combat operations on equal footing with their male counterparts. The relative risk of death or injury borne by men in combat arms and other positions most likely explains why men are overrepresented in the casualty statistics.[4] As of October 3, 2011, men accounted for 98 percent of the 4,468 military deaths in OIF and Operation New Dawn and for an equal percentage of the 1,675 military deaths in OEF. The gender ratio of the total physically wounded in these operations (31,922 and 13,011, respectively) is similar: Men account for 98 percent or more of those physically wounded (DMDC, 2011).

Because women's military roles have been evolving over the past decade, it makes sense for DoD to formally review its assignment policy to determine whether changes are in order. The last time such a review occurred was following the 1991 Gulf War.

Recent Interest in Limitations on Military Women's Roles

Despite an increase in the number and types of positions open to women since the advent of the all-volunteer force, gender restrictions continue to affect the types of positions military women can fill. The nature and needs of military operations in Iraq and Afghanistan, as well as the way women have been utilized, have attracted DoD and congressional attention to the issue. In response, several recent studies have focused explicitly on the effect of gender restrictions and the direct ground combat exclusion on opportunities for women. A 2006 RAND study for the Under Secretary of Defense for Personnel and Readiness examined how the direct ground combat and collocation exclusions were being applied in Army operations in Iraq and found that there were significant challenges in the interpretation and application of the DoD and Army assignment policies on the nonlinear battlefield (see Harrell, Castaneda, et al., 2007). These challenges were also driven by changes in the Army's organizational structure since 1994, which, in turn, affected how support and maneuver units were positioned and used. The report found that although commanders appeared to be complying with

---

4 The website icasualties.org compiles casualty data from news sources and public announcements and, to the degree possible, provides the name, service, unit, cause of death, and location for U.S. military personnel deaths in Iraq and Afghanistan.

the DoD direct ground combat exclusion, evidence of adherence to gender restrictions for collocated units (units that are physically located and remain with combat units) was more mixed, not due to intentional noncompliance but to inconsistencies and ambiguity in the policy (Harrell, Castaneda, et al. 2007). The report recommended redefining terms, such as *collocation*, that had been interpreted in different ways (proximity versus interdependence) and clarifying the intent of the collocation restriction.

The 2009 report of the Defense Advisory Committee on Women in the Services (DACOWITS) addressed the topic of the utilization of women in the OIF and OEF theaters of operation. In DACOWITS focus groups with 336 military personnel who had to deployed to OIF and/or OEF,

> The overwhelming majority of Service members indicated that women should be able to fill any and all roles in the military as long as they are capable and qualified for the job. . . . Military leaders were often unaware or uncertain of the current policy related to women serving in combat. Comments ranged from the policy being unfair or outdated, to not enforced (as women are currently serving in combat). (DACOWITS, 2010, p. 138)

DACOWITS found that military women serving in Iraq and Afghanistan had fired weapons and been fired upon, traveled in convoys, participated in female search teams (e.g., Lioness), and had been exposed to the risk of being fired upon simply because of the fluidity of the battlefield. Consequently, DACOWITS recommended additional combat-related training for all non–combat arms personnel, that the assignment policy for military women be reevaluated and changed, and that the recommendations in the 2007 RAND report be adopted across all the services (DACOWITS, 2010, p. 138).

The National Defense Authorization Act for Fiscal Year 2009 established the Military Leadership Diversity Commission (MLDC). As part of its deliberations, the MLDC considered the effect of gender restrictions on military women's employment opportunities and advancement to leadership positions. The commission's analyses found that women were underrepresented at both the senior noncommissioned officer (NCO) and flag/general officer levels and had significantly lower retention rates relative to their male counterparts (MLDC, 2011). The commission deemed the combat exclusion policies to be a significant structural barrier to the inclusion and advancement of women in the U.S. military. Specifically, it found that

> these policies work at two levels. First, they explicitly prohibit women from serving in certain tactical/operational career fields, such as infantry in the Army. Second, within the career fields that are open to women, the policies may prevent women from getting key assignments because they prohibit women from being assigned to units that are likely to be involved in direct offensive ground combat. (MLDC, 2011, p. 66)

In 2006, 80 percent of the Army's general officers came from combat arms occupations, all of which are closed to women (Lim et al., 2009).

The MLDC recommended that DoD and the services "eliminate combat exclusion policies for women, including removing barriers and inconsistencies, to create a level playing field for all servicemembers who meet the qualifications" (MLDC, 2011, p. xvii). The MLDC argued that it is unclear whether existing policies even apply on the nonlinear battlefield of the current conflicts and noted that women were already performing combat roles in Iraq and Afghanistan out of necessity. In addition to recommending a phased removal of barriers to female participation in direct ground combat units, the MLDC report recommended a standard set of strategic metrics to track the information about restrictions and opportunities for women across the services, as well as benchmarks to measure progress (MLDC, 2011, pp. 71–72, 101).

Reflecting continued interest in this issue, the National Defense Authorization Act for Fiscal Year 2011, Section 535, mandates that

> The Secretary of Defense, in coordination with the Secretaries of the military departments, shall conduct a review of laws, policies, and regulations, including the collocation policy, that may restrict the service of female members of the Armed Forces to determine whether changes in such laws, policies, and regulations are needed to ensure that female members have an equitable opportunity to compete and excel in the Armed Forces. (Pub. L. 111-383, 2011)

To accomplish this task, the Under Secretary of Defense for Personnel and Readiness initiated the Women in the Services Review (WISR), consisting of a senior-leader steering committee and a working group with representatives from the Air Force, Army, Marine Corps, and Navy. The data analyses presented here supported the WISR's preparation of its report to Congress; this report provides details about the current restrictions on women's service. The goal of this report is to document the military occupations that are closed to women, as well as occupations that are open to women but have some closed positions. Our efforts include providing, where possible, the service justification for the closures and quantifying the extent of these restrictions in the active components as of fiscal year 2011. For occupations in which some but not all positions are closed to women, we provide additional context by reporting the percentage of active-component women serving in those occupations as of December 2010. For a few sample occupations with some closed positions, we also explore the nature of the closures, possible implications for career progression, and additional details about the degree of the closures and women's representation by pay grade.

Organization of This Report

The remainder of the report looks more closely at the current implementation of the restrictions on women's military service, primarily as captured in service policy and administrative data. The purpose is to describe the positions that are unavailable to military women, not to debate the policies. Chapter Two describes the data and methods used in our analyses and explains terms used throughout the report. Chapter Three provides a brief overview of the results for all the services. Subsequent chapters offer overviews of the closures in each service: Chapter Four for the Air Force, Chapter Five for the Army, Chapter Six for the Marine Corps, and Chapter Seven for the Navy. Chapter Eight summarizes the findings. Based on issues we encountered while working with the services' data, that chapter also offers recommendations to the services to increase the transparency and accuracy of databases documenting service restrictions.

CHAPTER TWO

Terms, Data, and Methods

This study analyzed authorization and personnel data for active-component personnel in the U.S. Air Force, Army, Marine Corps, and Navy. The restrictions described here do not capture limitations on military women in the reserve components. It was also beyond the scope of this effort to report on restrictions in temporary duty assignments, such as Air Force constraints on female Airmen filling temporary duty assignments in Kuwait, Oman, Afghanistan, and Saudi Arabia.

This chapter outlines terms used commonly in this report and describes the data sets and other sources of information we used to determine the gender restrictions on women's military service.

Definition of Commonly Used Terms

Many different terms can be used to describe gender restrictions in the armed forces: Some are synonymous and others make important distinctions. To improve the accessibility of this report to the nonmilitary expert, we have reduced the amount of service-specific but comparable language by adopting some general terms. We have also attempted to reduce confusion that could arise from using many synonyms for particular terms by choosing to frequently repeat a few terms. Table 2.1 presents some of the most common and important terms used in this report, along with descriptions and illustrative examples.

Throughout this report we use the term *position* to describe a space in a unit that may or may not be open to women. Positions may be closed based on the occupation (also referred to as a career field) or the subspecialty within an occupation required to fill that position. Positions may also or instead be closed because of the type of unit in which they are located.

Table 2.1
Common Terms, with Descriptions and Examples

Term	Description	Examples
Occupation	Overarching term to refer to a line of work; "career field" is a synonym, as is "rating" for Navy enlisted personnel	Medicine, health care
Specialty	Subset of an occupation	Cardiologist, registered nurse, combat medic, X-ray technician
Additional skills	Specialized training, skills, or qualifications above those required for an occupational specialty	Parachutist, nuclear medicine, combat diving
Unit	Generic term for any military organization; it could range in size from a few people to tens of thousands and is located within a military hierarchy; units are made up of people serving in individual positions	Hospital, emergency room, clinic, medical lab, ship, wing, battalion, brigade
Position	A specific job in a specific unit, which typically must be filled by someone with a particular occupation, specialty, set of additional skills, and/or prior experience Also referred to as "billets" in all services except the Army	Command surgeon, U.S. Central Command, MacDill Air Force Base; Combat medic, 1st Special Troops Battalion, 1st Brigade Combat Team, 82nd Airborne Division, Fort Bragg
Authorizations/ authorized positions	Funded positions in a fiscal year; may not match actual number of people in positions	19,562 Army 68W health care specialists in fiscal year 2011
Closed occupations, units, positions	Occupations, units, or positions in which women cannot serve because of the 1994 policy, because women cannot obtain the necessary prerequisites or for other reasons	Hospital corpsman positions in Navy riverine boat teams, patrol craft, submarines, frigates, and Marine Corps units below the division level in the ground combat element

Limitations on the Ability to Match Closures to the Policy Rationales

The categories defined in the 1994 policy (direct ground combat, collocation, special operations/long-range reconnaissance, berthing/privacy, and physical job requirements) are relevant in terms of the extent and number of positions affected by restrictions. However, these closure categories are by no means mutually exclusive. For example, special operations positions may involve direct ground combat, require collocation with direct ground combat units, and have physical requirements that most women cannot meet.

Additionally, although none of the services reported in 1994 that any of its closures were due to the physical demands of the job, the ground combat force representatives in the 2011 WISR working group believe that this was because other justifications were already sufficient to close occupations with very heavy physical job requirements, not because that rationale did not also apply.

Table 2.2 shows a matrix of specialties and units, with codes reflecting the service responses to the 1994 policy memo. In most cases, only one rationale was offered, although occasionally there were two. The table also displays question marks where other restrictions might apply but were not documented in 1994. Air Force pararescue and Army ranger are special operations specialties; however, in 1994, the Air Force, Army, and Navy listed their special operations occupations under the direct ground combat exclusion rather than under the special operations exclusion. As part of the WISR, the services have indicated that the physical demands provision may also apply to some of the closed occupations but that additional review would be necessary to determine which ones. Thus, we have included question marks under that category to indicate that, despite the lack of documentation, the justification may have applied in 1994 as well.

The overlap in restriction categories illustrates why we do not report discrete, seemingly mutually exclusive counts of positions closed to women by each rationale.

Another hurdle to classifying all closed positions by rationale is that the way the services determined the rationales in 1994 does not necessarily apply today. First, the way all-male specialties and units are employed today may have changed since 1994, due to technological advances, military reorganization, or the demands of sustained counterinsurgency operations. Second, some specialties that existed in 1994 have been phased out or reclassified, and some specialties not identified in 1994 are among those

Table 2.2
Sample Matrix of How Restriction Rationales Match Closed Occupations and Units, Reflecting 1994 Service Codes and Other Possibly Relevant Codes Not Documented

Military Occupation or Unit	Direct Ground Combat	Collocation	Long-Range Reconnaissance/ Special Operations	Berthing/ Privacy	Physical Demands
Air Force pararescue	√		?		?
Army ranger	√		?		?
Army infantry	√				?
Marine Corps main battle tank repairer/ technician		√			?
Marine Corps interrogation platoon		√	√		
Navy sonar technician, submarine				√	

NOTE: √ = Rationale provided in 1994; ? = other possible rationale(s) not provided in 1994.

with closures today. Third, the specialties and units were not coded for every applicable rationale, so an inquiry of how many positions are closed due to which rationale may not produce the intended type of result. For example, a tally to capture positions closed under the special operations/reconnaissance rationale would miss most special operations and reconnaissance positions because, in 1994, the services designated them as closed due to the direct ground combat mission. Thus, although these codes were useful for determining which positions would remain closed, they offer limited insight into the full consideration of why a position is closed and whether removal of a given rationale would open that position or not.

We do have some current information about service justifications for closing positions. For the WISR, the Air Force provided rationale notes for its short list of positions with closures, many of which are in special operations specialties. Those notes specified the justifications as direct ground combat, assigned with infantry battalions, or in special operations/infantry battalions. The Army's Personnel Management Authorization Document (PMAD) database includes a single category that identifies whether a position is closed due to direct ground combat and/or collocation (yes or no). We have no information more recent than 1994 for Marine Corps closures. The Navy updated its assignment policy for women in 2011 (OPNAV Instruction 1300.17B), which includes a list of assignments closed to women and a code indicating the applicable rationale. In the Navy, the majority of closures are due to limited berthing and privacy arrangements, most commonly on submarines. Special operations closures are justified due to the direct ground combat mission; the physical requirements justification was never used. The SEAL delivery vehicle team technician was the only Navy specialty listed as closed due to the collocation policy and also the only specialty with a closure justified by more than one rationale (it is also closed due to direct ground combat).

To draw a broader picture of how the 1994 policy provisions on gender restrictions (e.g., direct ground combat, berthing/privacy) affect assignment opportunities for women across the services, we relied on a number of data sources, both qualitative and quantitative.

Service and DoD Policies

Service assignment policies assisted us in understanding which positions are closed and why. The Air Force assignment policy, Air Force Instruction 36-2110 (2009), lists no Air Force units closed to women. It is the Army's policy or interpretation of policy that governs whether Air Force positions in Army units are open to women. Army Regulation 600-13 (1992) defines direct combat and collocation as they apply in the Army case, identifies the decision process used to code positions as open or closed to women, and describes the types of restrictions that affect the positions open to women. Chapter 5 of the Marine Corps personnel assignment policy, Marine Corps

Order P1300.8R (1994), provides guidance on the assignment of women and lists closed career fields, MOSs, and units, although a few of the MOSs are now out of date. The Navy's recently revised policy, OPNAV Instruction 1300.17B (2011), describes the specialties and vessels that are closed to female enlisted personnel and officers and clarifies the positions from which they are not excluded.

In addition to these assignment policy documents, we also considered other instructions and memoranda that are relevant to gender policy and gender restrictions. These include the initial policy statement by Secretary of Defense Aspin, the required inputs provided by each service in 1994, letters submitted to Congress by the Secretary of Defense reporting the intention to open certain occupations and vessels to women, and policies that govern requirements for berthing and sanitation facilities on ships.

Authorization Data

"Spaces and faces" is a common expression in DoD for describing two types of data. "Spaces" refers to positions, or job openings within units that ultimately may or may not be filled in a given year. Funded, available spaces are referred to as "authorizations" or "authorized positions" and are quantified in the services' "authorizations data." "Faces" refers to actual people serving in the military who can be assigned to fill those spaces within the units. This report draws extensively on the data for spaces, or authorized positions.

Active-component authorization data for each service include detailed information about each funded position, including unit/location, rank, career field or occupational specialty, and prerequisite skills. Because authorization data do not include information on individuals, only "spaces" that can be filled by personnel, they do not reflect the total number of active-component personnel, which could fall above or below the number of authorizations. In fiscal year 2011, the number of personnel, or *end strength*, exceeded the number of authorizations, which is permissible under U.S. Code Title 10, Section 123a, during a time of war or national emergency.

Authorization data are essential to the analyses presented here because they allowed us to identify open and closed positions in occupations and units. Each service's authorization data are organized and coded differently, particularly when it comes to gender restrictions.

Because this study focused on describing and quantifying occupations completely closed to women, as well as occupations with some closed positions, we did not use the portion of the authorization files that includes allotments for military personnel who are patients, prisoners, students, trainees, transient between positions, or otherwise not assigned to jobs. Marine Corps manpower analysts, as part of the WISR, compared the overall results using the portion of the authorization data that we used, with the results we would have obtained if we had also included the 32,635 authorizations for Marines not assigned to jobs. The difference in results is worth noting: Using the data containing positions only, the results show that 68 percent of jobs are open to female Marines. If prisoners, patients, trainees, and transients (P2T2) are included, however, it appears that 73 percent of Marine Corps positions are open, because those authorizations do not denote any gender exclusions.

For the Air Force, we used the March 2011 Air Force Authorized Manpower Master (MPW), which did not contain information on gender restrictions. Career field managers and the Air Force representatives to the WISR provided the information we needed to code the 1 percent of positions that are closed to female Airmen. The career field managers who match personnel to positions are responsible for knowing which positions are closed to women.

For the Army, the authorization data came from the March 2011 PMAD. All positions in the PMAD are coded to indicate whether they can be filled by men only, women only, or men and women. We used this coding to determine which military occupational specialties (MOSs) that are open to women have some positions that are closed and in which units or locations those closures occur. The PMAD data indicate closed positions based on the application of the Army's Direct Combat Probability Coding (DCPC), a binary coding reflecting routine engagement in direct ground combat or routine collocation with direct combat units (closed to women) or the lack of such engagement or collocation (open to women). The code does not distinguish between closures due to routine direct ground combat and closures due to routine collocation with direct ground combat units.

Had we relied solely on DCPC in the PMAD, however, we would have missed thousands of positions closed to women not because of direct combat or collocation but because women are unable to fill the prerequisite occupations. The authorization data identify the rank and occupation required to fill a position. In the Army data, the DCPC code also identifies whether the position is closed to women. So, the PMAD DCPC data column might suggest that female lieutenant colonels could fill armor leadership positions at the brigade level, because those positions do not routinely engage in direct ground combat or collocate with units that do. But those positions are also coded as needing to be filled by an officer in the armor career field, which is closed to women. Because the occupation required to fill these leadership positions is closed to women, these positions are effectively closed to women. In our tabulations, if women cannot become qualified to fill a position, we consider it closed to women, even if the PMAD DCPC data do not explicitly code the position as closed to women.

The Marine Corps authorization data come from the January 2011 Total Force Structure Management System (TFSMS). In that database, each position is coded as open to men only, open to women only, or open to either gender. This system both provides visibility to Marine Corps leadership on the location and extent of closures and allows the personnel who match Marines to assignments to know where they should and should not place female Marines. At the time of this review, the Marine Corps was in the process of identifying and correcting errors in the TFSMS gender data field. Therefore, WISR representatives used the Marine Corps assignment policy to code the authorization data for us according to whether the positions were open to men or women, closed to women because the MOS is closed, or closed to women because the unit is closed. The data in this report reflect the number of authorizations recorded in the TFSMS and the gender coding provided by the WISR representatives.

Like the Air Force, the Navy's authorization data do not include information on gender restrictions. The magnitude of closures, however, was much greater in the Navy data than in the Air Force data. The June 2011 data we used came from the Total Force Manpower Management System (TFMMS) and include unit and ship information, rating and Naval Enlisted Classification (NEC) occupational codes for enlisted personnel, and designator and billet codes for officers.[1] For specialties that the policy defined as entirely closed to women, it was relatively straightforward to identify and quantify the number and types of positions. A Navy manpower analyst and Navy representatives from the Office of Women's Policy, the submarine and special warfare communities, the hospital corpsman enlisted rating, and Riverine Group 1 helped decipher unit names and distinguish open from closed positions in Navy and Marine Corps units to which Sailors are assigned. The coding required these inquiries because it was not simply the case that all positions in special warfare, riverine, or Marine Corps units are closed. Instead, closures affect only certain positions based on their location and duties. Because the authorization data do not indicate which positions are closed to women, the detailers must know and apply Navy policies when assigning Sailors to positions.

For each service, the authorization data lacked information indicating individual commander requests for a position to be filled by a man or a woman only.

Most of this report and its appendixes reflect the use of the authorization data, because they were the source of the information about the number and types of positions available and not available to women.

DEERS PITE Personnel Data

Personnel data files provide information about the "faces," or actual people serving in the military. These files offer some context for understanding the positions that are closed to women, although there are limits to the conclusions that can be drawn from them.

[1] Ratings and NEC codes are both ways of classifying the occupations of Navy enlisted personnel. A rating is a broad career field, such as machinist's mate or sonar technician. An NEC code references a specific job. One NEC code may be associated with one or more ratings. For officers, a designator specifies a job, whereas a Naval Officer Billet Code represents specific technical skills or qualifications required for that job.

The December 2010 Defense Manpower Data Center Defense Enrollment Eligibility Reporting System Point in Time Extracts (DEERS PITE) data provided a snapshot of active-component service members from the four services. In contrast to authorization data, these data represent individuals, not job positions. Thus, they also include trainees, students, transients, patients, and prisoners—everyone in the active component. "Active component" does not encompass guard and reserve members mobilized on active duty. These numbers will fluctuate daily as people enter and leave the active component and as people move from specialty to specialty through (1) lateral moves, e.g., from the Army's enlisted 12B combat engineer to its enlisted 88M motor transport operator; (2) moves that reflect career progression within a rank group, such as from the Army's enlisted 12B to 12Z combat engineering senior sergeant; or (3) promotion from the enlisted ranks and specialties into warrant officer or officer ranks and specialties.

For this study, we used the DEERS PITE variables on gender, occupational specialty, career field, and pay grade to identify where women are concentrated and where women are scarce. In Chapter Three, which provides an overview of our results, we use these data to show the distribution of women across the services by rank group. We also used the DEERS PITE data to quantify the percentage of military women serving in open specialties that have some closed positions, which are presented in the tables in Appendixes B and C (in the columns labeled "Percentage of Positions Filled by Women"). Coupled with the authorization data for open occupations, we can compare the percentage of positions open to women to the percentage of positions filled by women. In occupations with 60 percent of positions open to women, there is greater competition for open positions if women make up 30 percent of an occupation than if women make up 2 percent. Moreover, these constraints are greater in smaller occupations in which there are relatively few positions available in the first place. We cannot conclude, however, that the percentage of positions open to women entirely explains the number of women in the occupations (i.e., the percent of positions filled by women). Many factors contribute to whether women enter and remain in military occupations. Assignment opportunities may be an important factor, but they are not necessarily the most important or determining factor. Similarly, we cannot conclude that the decline in military women's representation at the senior pay grades is explained by the restrictions on women's service. Other factors can play a role in the retention and promotion of military women.

Occupational Guides

The occupational guides for each service allowed us to match occupational codes in the authorization and personnel data sets with titles and occupational or career fields, as well as to investigate job requirements and descriptions. These job descriptions can provide insight into the rationale for gender restrictions on certain positions by explaining, for example, that they are specific to submarines or special operations, or that they have prerequisite or additional skill requirements for which women are ineligible. The Air Force Specialty Code (AFSC) guide helped us understand how the closed positions related to the larger occupations in which they were set. The Army's MOS guide, Pamphlet 611-21 (HQDA, 2007), describes each occupation in detail and includes information about mental and physical job demands. Current occupational codes and titles were provided by the Army. The Marine Corps MOS manual allowed us to distinguish primary MOSs (PMOSs) from the free MOSs that Marines with any primary MOS can hold and exception MOSs, which can be filled only by Marines with certain PMOSs. Where the guides map out the career trajectory for specific occupational fields, as in the Navy enlisted guide, they allowed us to consider how restrictions might affect career advancement.

Other Information Provided by the Services

Service representatives provided additional data and information to the WISR or to us as part of the WISR effort. As an example, the Navy provided data on enlisted berthing designated specifically for men and specifically for women. The Marine Corps shared the information it was reviewing on job-related physical demands. Each of the services also responded to questions about data, processes, and policies. Career field managers helped us better understand a subset of specialties and careers. Service feedback on drafted tables and narratives also helped improve the accuracy and clarity of this report.

Conclusion

This chapter explained how our analyses focused on quantifying the positions that are closed to women, whether those positions are closed because the occupation required to fill the positions is closed or because the unit in which they are located is closed. There may be more than one policy rationale for closing a position. Not all documented rationales for position closures are current or indicate all rationales that apply to each position. Still, this report describes positions that are closed under provisions of the 1994 policy.

The remainder of this report provides information about the percentage of positions closed to military women in each service. We analyzed fiscal year 2011 authorized position data files and 2010 personnel files, consulted service occupational guides, and reviewed other documentation and communicated with service representatives. The numbers and percentages presented here represent a snapshot in time: The composition of authorized positions changes over time, as does the composition of the force.

CHAPTER THREE

Overview of Results

This chapter provides a brief overview of the percentage of women serving in the armed forces, by service and rank group, and summarizes the degree to which fiscal year 2011 authorized positions are open to them. Subsequent chapters discuss closures by service and provide more information about the variation in restrictions by occupation and unit.

Representation of Women in the Active-Component Military

Many factors influence the representation of men and women in the military, including eligibility, level of interest in joining and remaining in the military, preferences for particular jobs or services, service recruiting and retention efforts, ability to meet physical standards, compatibility of military service with family life, leadership and work climate (e.g., mentoring, harassment, discrimination), job satisfaction and opportunities for career advancement, and competing civilian opportunities.

More than 80 percent of military personnel are men, but there is variability in the representation of women across the services and through the ranks of officers, warrant officers, and enlisted personnel (see Table 3.1). The percentage of women is highest in the Air Force (19 percent), followed by the Navy (16 percent), the Army (13 percent), and the Marine Corps (7 percent). In each service, women's representation is greatest in the entry-level rank groups (O1–O3 pay grades for officers and E1–E4 pay grades for enlisted personnel).

Overview of Gender Restrictions Across the Services

Before providing detail about the specific types of positions closed to military women, we offer summary tabulations by service and rank group. Table 3.2 shows the percentage of authorized positions closed to women because of the permissible restrictions of collocation, direct ground combat, privacy and berthing, special operations, or long-range reconnaissance; because the restrictions prevent women from meeting the posi-

Table 3.1
Representation of Military Women in the Active Component, by Service and Rank Group

	Air Force		Army		Marine Corps		Navy	
Rank Group	**Total Number of Personnel**	**% Women**	**Total Number of Personnel**	**% Women**	**Total Number of Personnel**	**% Women**	**Total Number of Personnel**	**% Women**
O7–O10	316	8	334	5	89	1	257	9
O4–O6	28,813	15	32,101	14	6,559	4	20,954	13
O1–O3	37,893	22	49,046	20	13,154	7	30,501	18
All officers	67,022	19	81,481	17	19,802	6	51,712	16
Warrant officers	NA	NA	16,035	9	1,987	5	1,633	5
E7–E9	33,905	15	58,597	11	14,818	5	29,762	8
E5–E6	112,525	20	150,721	12	47,212	7	114,213	14
E1–E4	119,049	20	270,528	14	119,888	7	131,364	20
All enlisted	264,473	19	479,846	13	181,918	7	275,339	16
All active component	332,502	19	577,362	13	203,707	7	328,684	16

SOURCE: DEERS PITE, December 2010.

Table 3.2
Number of Active-Component Authorized Positions, Percentage of Positions Open to Women, and Percentage Filled by Women, by Service and Rank Group

Service	Rank Group	Number of Active-Component Authorized Positions	Percentage of Authorized Positions Open to Women
Air Force	Officer	58,716	99.6[a]
	Enlisted	241,136	99
	Total	299,852	99
Army	Officer	67,046	81
	Warrant	13,726	90
	Enlisted	394,730	63
	Total	475,502	66
Marine Corps	Officer	15,482	78
	Warrant	2,176	86
	Enlisted	151,807	67
	Total	169,465	68
Navy	Officer	44,030	95
	Warrant	1,588	88
	Enlisted	236,125	86
	Total	281,743	88

SOURCE: Percentages of authorized positions open to women were derived from service authorization data for fiscal year 2011. The table excludes patients, students, trainees, prisoners, and personnel in transition and thus does not equal end strength.

[a] Not rounded to avoid the impression that all positions are open.

tion prerequisites; or because those positions were, for other reasons, designated in the data sets as "male only."

Among the services, the Air Force has the greatest percentage of authorized positions open to women (99 percent). The Air Force does not have warrant officer ranks. Although the Army has the largest number of positions and the Marine Corps has the smallest, the percentage of authorized positions open to female soldiers (66 percent) is similar to the percentage of authorized positions open to female Marines (68 percent). These are the two services that are primarily responsible for conducting direct ground combat operations. In the Navy, 88 percent of authorized positions are open to women. Across the Army, Marine Corps, and Navy, the percentage of positions open to women is higher for officers than for enlisted personnel.

The total authorized positions in Table 3.2 are broken into two columns in Table 3.3 according to whether they are in specialties closed to women or in specialties open to women. The rightmost column reflects the number of authorized positions that appear in specialties open to women but are closed because those positions are in units that are closed to women. In the case of the Navy, the term *unit* includes vessels (patrol craft, ships, and submarines) on which women, predominantly enlisted women, cannot serve due to berthing limitations.

For the Air Force, Army, and Marine Corps, overall, the number of closed positions in closed occupational specialties is greater than the number of closed positions in specialties open to women. By rank group and by service, however, that is not always true—or at least not to the same degree. In particular, for Army officers and Marine Corps warrant officers, the difference is not as great, and for Army warrant officers, there are more closed positions in the open occupations. For the Navy, the concentration of closures among open occupations for enlisted women is a function of the

Table 3.3
Number of Active-Component Authorized Positions in Specialties Closed and Open to Women and Number of Closed Positions in Open Specialties, by Service and Rank Group

Service	Rank Group	Number of Authorized Positions in Closed Specialties	Number of Authorized Positions in Open Specialties	Number of Closed Positions in Open Specialties[a]
Air Force	Officer	214	58,502	14
	Enlisted	2,934	238,202	69
	Total	3,148	296,704	83
Army	Officer	6,586	60,460	6,378
	Warrant	567	13,159	770
	Enlisted	116,826	277,904	28,769
	Total	123,979	351,523	35,917
Marine Corps	Officer	2,793	12,689	595
	Warrant	184	1,992	121
	Enlisted	35,932	115,875	14,096
	Total	38,909	130,556	14,812
Navy	Officer	991	43,039	1,068
	Warrant	175	1,413	8
	Enlisted	7,062	229,063	25,518
	Total	8,228	273,515	26,594

[a] A subset of the previous column.

number of positions on ships that are closed to enlisted women, which we will address in greater depth later.

Conclusion

Military women make up the highest percentage of the force in the Air Force, followed, in order, by the Navy, the Army, and the Marine Corps. The percentage of positions open to military women also follows that order, although we do not have evidence that would permit us to claim that one causes the other: Many factors can influence the gender ratio in the armed forces. The variation seen in the number and percentages of positions closed to women (Tables 3.2 and 3.3) can be understood by looking more closely at which positions are closed to women and why, which is the focus of the following chapters.

CHAPTER FOUR

Air Force Positions Closed to Women

Ninety-nine percent of Air Force positions are open to female Airmen, and the description of closures is relatively straightforward. It describes the occupations in which all positions are closed to women and the occupations that have some gender-based restrictions. We provide alphanumeric AFSCs for the named occupations for those who wish to look up detailed data in Appendixes A and B.

Closed Occupations

All of the 3,148 authorized positions in closed occupations in the Air Force are special operations positions. Closed Air Force officer occupations are 13DXA combat rescue officer and 13DXB special tactics officer; closed enlisted occupations are 1C2X1 combat controller, 1C4X1 tactical air control party, 1T2X1 pararescue, and 1W0X2 special operations weather. Table A.1 in Appendix A provides details on the number of authorized positions for each occupation individually. Known collectively as battlefield Airmen, personnel in these occupations are typically embedded in Army, Navy, or Marine Corps special operations units to control air fire support, provide weather support, or offer medical and rescue assistance (Feickert, 2011).

Open Occupations with Some Closed Positions

In the few Air Force occupations that are open but have restrictions on the assignment of women, more than 97 percent of positions are open to women (see Table B.1 in Appendix B). Positions in special operations units are closed to female officers in the 15W weather specialty. The enlisted occupation 3D1X3 radio frequency transmission systems has some closures based on the expectation that these Airmen would be assigned to Army infantry battalions. Because they have been serving in Army brigades and thus have not been collocated with or involved in direct ground combat missions, these positions are likely to open to the assignment of women.

Air Liaison Officers

The Air Force defers to the Army's policy when its personnel are assigned to Army units. Air liaison officers (ALOs) lead Tactical Air Control Party and Air Support Operations Center operations, collocating with Army infantry units to help coordinate air, ground, and space assets on the battlefield. "Air liaison officer" is both a type of assignment and a new occupation. It is an assignment that pilots (11XXU), combat systems officers (12XXU, navigators), and remotely piloted aircraft pilots (18AXU) can fill, but they have the option to return to service in other pilot and navigator positions. Since 2009, ALO is also an officer career field (13LX). Female Air Force officers do serve in ALO positions and may find a career path to command opportunities by doing so. Women may not serve at the battalion level in the Army's infantry units. The Army has been placing ALOs at the brigade level, however, rather than collocating them with units whose primary mission is direct ground combat. All funded authorizations as of July 2011 were at the brigade level and above, and ALO career field managers did not foresee any change to this practice. However, should the Army choose to place ALOs in the infantry battalions, those positions would be closed under the current policy. Few women serve in the ALO positions.

Conclusion

Relatively few positions are closed to Air Force women. All closed occupations are special operations occupations. Most gender restrictions in open occupations are the result of the Army's assignment policy, which applies to Air Force personnel assigned to Army units. Since those positions have been located in Army infantry brigades, rather than the closed infantry battalions, the assignment policy has not closed them to women. All positions in other active-component Air Force occupations not listed here are open to women.

CHAPTER FIVE

Army Positions Closed to Women

In contrast to the Air Force, the number of Army gender restrictions is extensive due to the centrality of direct ground combat in its organizational mission. This chapter provides an overview of the occupations that are closed to Army women. A detailed list of those occupations and their authorized positions is provided in Table A.2 in Appendix A. This chapter also discusses occupations that are open but have some closed positions; detailed information on that even lengthier list is presented in Tables B.2–B.4 in Appendix B. An overview of the career field of military intelligence explores how the closures are distributed across pay grades.

Closed Occupations

The Army has the largest number of positions of any service in occupations that are closed to women (123,979). This is the product of having the large number of personnel and a ground combat focus. Nearly half of these closures are in the infantry branch (61,594). The largest Army officer occupation closed to women is 11A infantry, with 3,744 positions. The largest enlisted Army occupation closed to women—11B infantryman—is also the largest occupation in DoD that is closed to women, with 50,518 authorized positions. The armor career field, involving the operation and maintenance of tanks and Bradley fighting vehicles, also has a large number of positions (19,736 positions). Special forces occupations are closed to women as well and account for 7,482 positions. The five active-duty special forces groups are involved in reconnaissance, intelligence, and rescue operations, as well as covert infiltrations on the ground and using airborne assets (Feickert, 2011).

These figures include positions that were not marked in the authorization data as "closed" because, as an Army representative explained, they do not meet the criteria for direct ground combat as a primary mission. For example, the authorization data typically did not indicate that 11A infantry officer positions at the brigade level or above were closed to women. The positions are coded this way so that there are brigade-level leaders commanding infantry battalions who have infantry occupation training, experience, and knowledge and so that infantry officers have assignments available as they progress beyond the battalion level. Technically, brigade-level infantry positions would be open to women because they involve overseeing direct ground combat units rather than participating in direct ground combat. But because women cannot enter the infantry occupation needed to fill those positions, we coded them as closed. This was consistent with the Marine Corps' coding of its authorizations data. Any comparison of our tabulations with other tabulations of Army authorization data should take into account this possible variation in how a "closed position" is defined.

Positions Closed Solely Because of the Collocation Restriction

Thousands of positions in closed Army occupations are closed due to the direct ground combat collocation restriction. In an April 2011 memorandum, Secretary of the Army John M. McHugh identified six Army occupations that are closed solely because of the collocation rationale. These occupations are as follows:

- three of the eight currently closed occupations in the field artillery branch:
  - 13M Multiple Launch Rocket System (MLRS) crewmember
  - 13P MLRS operations/fire direction specialist
  - 13R field artillery firefinder radar operator
- all three mechanical maintenance occupations:
  - 91A M1 Abrams tank system maintainer
  - 91M Bradley fighting vehicle system maintainer
  - 91P artillery mechanic.

The memorandum reports that the collocation restriction on military women also applies to positions in more than 80 units in MLRS, high-mobility artillery rocket systems, area clearance platoons, headquarters sections of clearance companies, and opposing forces in training battalions. The memorandum states that approximately 13,000 positions would open to women if the collocation restriction were lifted. MOSs that would have additional positions open to women as a result of such a change are field artillery, air defense, signal corps, electronic warfare, maintenance, military intelligence, psychological operations, civil affairs, and public affairs. Thus, more than just the six closed occupations would be affected by this change.

We looked at the Army's 1994 list of occupations closed under the collocation rationale to identify additional implications of the elimination of the collocation restriction. In 1994, the Army reported that air defense artillery (short-range air defense), ground surveillance radar, combat engineering (enlisted MOS 12B), and MLRS would remain closed to women due to collocation. No air defense artillery occupations will open as a result of lifting the collocation restriction because, in 2011, no air defense artillery specialty was still closed to women. Ground surveillance radar no longer exists as an MOS. The enlisted 12B combat engineering specialty does still exist, is still closed, and is large (10,158 positions). Army WISR representatives report that this MOS has since been reclassified as closed due to the direct ground combat assignment rule.

Open Occupations with Some Closed Positions

The 35,917 closed positions in open occupations usually either are located in closed units or have prerequisites that are closed to women, such as prior experience in closed occupations or additional skills or qualifications closed to women. There are a few exceptions, however, in which a position was coded in the authorization data as "male only" but we were not able to discern why.

Closed Units

Female soldiers are excluded from permanent assignment to Army positions in units below the brigade level that have direct ground combat or special operations as a primary mission. Examples of closed units include maneuver battalions, cannon battalions, reconnaissance squadrons, sapper and other engineer companies, special operations aviation battalions, special forces battalions, ranger battalions, anti-armor companies, and long-range surveillance units. There is evidence, however, that women in support occupations have opportunities to serve "attached" or otherwise routinely interact with direct ground combat units in theater, even though they are not technically "assigned" to them (DACOWITS, 2010; Harrell, Castaneda, et al., 2007).

A large percentage of positions closed to women in open occupations are found in specialties in the medical corps, chemical corps, signal corps, intelligence, and motor transport career fields (see Table C.1 in Appendix C for details). There are differences in the scope of these restrictions and their effect on the number of positions that are closed to women. In the electronic warfare career field, for instance, only 57 percent of positions are open to women, but the entire career field has only 382 positions for all ranks combined. In contrast, 85 percent of positions in the signal corps branch and 88 percent of military intelligence positions are open, but the number of positions closed to women in each case is large: 4,988 and 2,999 positions, respectively. Army gender restrictions pertaining to direct ground combat units have very different implications for the officer, warrant officer, and enlisted rank groups.

Officer occupations with more than 2,000 authorized positions each and with some positions that are closed are as follows:

- 90A logistics (98 percent open)
- 25A signal, general (89 percent open)
- 35D all-source intelligence (86 percent open)
- 02A combat arms generalist, drawn from other occupations (78 percent open)
- 13A field artillery (33 percent open).

Officer specialties with the greatest limitations include field artillery, listed above, and the smaller occupations of 65D physician's assistant (71 percent of 809 positions open) and 70B health services administration (63 percent of 550 positions open).

Authorizations may end up being under- or overfilled. Women may have fewer assignment options if not all authorized positions can be filled, because the direct ground combat units closed to women are likely to be among the top priorities for receiving personnel; thus, the percentage of actual positions open to women may be lower than the authorization data reflect. Additionally, women's ability to compete for higher-level commands could be compromised by not having had the experience of their male counterparts who have served in direct ground combat units.

Most of the Army warrant officer occupations affected by closures have 90 percent or more assignments open to either gender. The exceptions are 254A signal system support technician (87 percent open), 290A electronic warfare (79 percent open), and 740A chemical, biological, radiological, and nuclear (CBRN) warrant officer (67 percent open, but with only 12 total authorizations).

Enlisted occupations with closures also range in overall size and the percentages of authorizations that are closed to women. The largest enlisted MOSs, with more than 10,000 positions, are

- 88M motor transport operator (99 percent open)
- 92A automated logistical specialist (97 percent open)
- 91B wheeled vehicle repairer (96 percent open)
- 42A human resources specialist (84 percent open)
- 92Y unit supply specialist (72 percent open)
- 68W health care specialist (66 percent).

The health care specialist MOS is the largest of all those MOSs and has the greatest degree of gender constraints: One in three of 19,562 positions can be filled only by men.

Some enlisted MOSs have small numbers of authorizations and significant restrictions, greatly constraining the assignment of women. Examples of these limitations in MOSs with fewer than 1,000 positions include the following:

- 94M radar repairer (57 percent open)
- 29E electronic warfare specialist (44 percent open)
- 13T field artillery surveyor/meteorological crewmember (12 percent open)
- 13Z field artillery senior sergeant (47 percent open).

The one entry-level field artillery position open to women (13T) involves monitoring weather conditions and placement of the artillery systems to ensure the accurate and lethal delivery of munitions and missiles. As the other field artillery MOSs are closed to enlisted women, and 88 percent of positions are closed to women in this one entry-level MOS (13T), it is perhaps not surprising that only 0.5 percent of 13Z field artillery senior sergeants as of December 2010 were women. This level of representation is similar to that in the 13Z senior sergeant MOS in 1998 (Beckett and Chien, 2002). The units that will open when the collocation exclusion is lifted will likely expand the number of positions open to women in field artillery.

To elaborate on how unit closures can vary by pay grade, we explored the example of officers in the military intelligence corps.

Army Military Intelligence

The officer intelligence profession offers an illustrative example of how closures due to collocation with direct ground combat units intersect with a career path. Women account for 20 percent of the 35D all-source intelligence area, the entry-level occupation and the core of the military intelligence field for officers. Officers in this specialty can be assigned to positions designated for other intelligence specialties, such as 35E counterintelligence. For all-source intelligence officers, the percentage of positions open to women increases as pay grade increases:

- 68 percent of first lieutenant (O2) positions
- 83 percent of captain (O3) positions
- 99 percent of major (O4) positions
- 99 percent of lieutenant colonel (O5)
- 100 percent of colonel (O6) positions.

The closed positions are concentrated early in the career, in junior officer tactical assignments at the battalion level or below. Majors serve at the brigade level, which is generally open to women. Overall, 86 percent of the 2,738 authorized positions in all-source intelligence are open to officer women, but that overall figure hides the degree to which junior officer assignment opportunities are constrained and the degree to which those constraints dissipate if women are able to—and choose to—remain in that career.

A career field manager for the military intelligence corps explained that it is important to distinguish between the most competitive career path for advancement and the most desired career path from the point of view of an officer. The most competitive career path involves a mix of tactical assignments, strategic assignments like those acquired at a brigade, and special assignments, such as serving as a recruiter or working in the equal opportunity office. The tactical assignments entail serving as the lone intelligence officer in a battalion, which, according to the career field manager, some junior officers find to be a difficult and high-pressure assignment. The career field manager reported that the infantry units are a heavily motorized force, meaning that they carry their gear and travel in vehicles, but that there are still physical demands above those of many other assignments. In the past, and potentially in the future, these intelligence positions in infantry units that are closed to women could require marching and carrying heavy packs. Regardless, the living conditions are often more austere than those at the brigade level or in non–combat arms units.

An important lesson from this career field is that the fastest-moving career option may not be the most desirable: Service members may prefer career paths that progress more slowly but allow for greater day-to-day job satisfaction or better work-life balance. Some intelligence officers have told career field managers that they prefer brigade-level assignments, where they serve with a group of other military intelligence officers and experience a lower level of stress. Indeed, the requirements branch of the Army Human Resources Command reports that, due to the number of deployments, there is a trend among officers to request Army Intelligence and Security Command or other nondeployable assignments to provide stability for the family and deployment recovery for the soldier. According to Army Human Resources Command, these positions are not only among the most requested, they are also among the most prestigious, as are joint assignments, positions with the national-level intelligence agencies, special mission units, and Human Resources Command. The demand for personnel and the job security in this career field have been sufficient that junior officers short on tactical assignments can succeed in being promoted if their performance in the assignments they do have is high. A representative from Human Resources Command reports that, relative to positions in all-male units, similar jobs in other units

> provide female Soldiers with the same experience, technical and leadership opportunities. Promotions for both male and female Soldiers who have not been assigned to units with only male coded positions are consistent with those male Soldiers who have been assigned to male only units.

Given that Army units at battalion level and below that are led by junior officers account for most of the units closed to Army women, the decline in formal policy-specified gender restrictions affecting women's career paths that we observed in this career field is likely repeated in other officer occupations. According to the personnel files, women's representation in 35D declines with advancement, from 24 percent of officers in pay grades O1–O3 to 13 percent in the higher pay grades, but that drop cannot be attributed to a lower percentage of positions being formally open to women at those higher levels because, on the contrary, a greater percentage are.

Positions with Prerequisites Closed to Women

There were a few exceptions to the rule that closed positions in open occupations fall at the battalion level or below. For example, 36A financial manager positions at the ranger regiment and the special operations aviation regiment are closed, and in the ranger regiment, a 420A human resources technician warrant officer position is closed, too. The impact of these limitations on women in these occupations is minute: Fully 99 percent of financial manager positions are open to officer women, as are

99.7 percent of the human resources positions. Other anomalies were noted, but these also generally accounted for less than 1 percent of authorized positions in any occupation.

These exceptions can occur if a position is designated as requiring an additional skill for which women cannot qualify. Then, that position will effectively be closed to women. Additional skills or qualifications that are closed to women include ranger, ranger parachutist, special forces sniper, special forces underwater operations, special forces military free-fall operations, and special forces combat diving: All are associated with combat operations.

General Officers

Nearly 10 percent of the 390 positions in the occupational category for general officers (02A) were designated to be filled by men only. The closed positions included commanding general positions in the active Army divisions and corps.

Conclusion

The greatest number of positions closed to military women are located in the Army, the largest service. Most closed positions are located in occupations closed to women, primarily infantry but also armor, field artillery, special forces, combat engineers, and mechanical maintenance. Six specialties in field artillery and mechanical maintenance are closed solely because of the collocation restriction.

Positions in open occupations that are closed to women are typically located in ground combat units at or below the battalion level. These closures affect a wide range of occupations to varying degrees. Because the types of units that are closed are led by junior officers, women who reach the rank of major and higher are likely to find that the number of positions closed to them diminishes. A greater percentage of open positions does not mean that women are equally competitive for promotion, command, or key assignments, however.[1] Although occupation and unit closures explain nearly all of the positions unavailable to Army women, some exceptions are noted.

---

1 For analyses of military women's promotion and career opportunities, see Asch, Miller, and Malchiado, forthcoming; GAO, 1998a; and Hosek et al., 2001.

CHAPTER SIX

Marine Corps Positions Closed to Women

The Marine Corps also has a large number of positions closed to women. This chapter provides an overview of the occupations that are closed to Marine Corps women. Tabular data about those occupations are presented in Table A.3 in Appendix A. This chapter also discusses open occupations that have some closed positions. Details are presented in Tables B.5–B.7 in Appendix B. A discussion about the communications field illustrates how the closures vary across specialties and rank groups.

Closed Occupations

As in the Army, the infantry career field accounts for the majority of the 38,909 positions in occupations closed to women in the Marine Corps. Authorized positions in closed career fields are represented by

- all 28,520 infantry positions
- all 4,669 field artillery positions
- all 2,886 tank and assault amphibious vehicle positions
- 1,876 of the ground ordnance maintenance positions
- 958 positions in other MOSs.

The largest officer occupation that is closed to women is 0302 infantry (1,587 positions). More than a third of all authorized positions in closed occupations (14,416) are in the enlisted 0311 rifleman specialty. Although all Marines, male and female, receive basic infantry skills training to prepare them to be riflemen first and foremost, the rifleman occupation is dedicated to mastering those skills and missions.

Some of the closed occupations focus on special operations. The Marine Corps Forces Special Operations Command is a relatively new creation (2005), but it is growing rapidly and will include about 3,000 Marines by 2014 (Feickert, 2011). Marine special operations units conduct long-range reconnaissance, infiltration, rescue, and other types of operations. They draw heavily from the infantry and require Marines to master additional skills, such as parachutist and combat diver qualifications. Authorization data show that positions for the enlisted occupation 0321 reconnaissance man (1,428) are frequently located within special operations units.

In response to direction for the services to open more positions to military women, in 2010, the Marine Corps opened two military intelligence MOSs:

- 0210 counterintelligence and human-source intelligence operations officer
- 0211 counterintelligence and human-source intelligence operations specialist (Marine Corps Administrative Message 026/11, 2011).

The positions in the 0210 officer MOS have no gender restrictions, and, in 0211, 99.9 percent of enlisted MOS positions are now open.

Open Occupations with Some Closed Positions

Marine Corps units below the division level in the "ground combat element" and low-altitude air defense battalions are closed to female Marines and Sailors in occupations open to them. The ground combat element includes infantry, artillery, tank, amphibious assault, and light armored reconnaissance battalions and infantry regiments. Overall, the Marine Corps career fields most heavily affected by unit-based gender restrictions, with about a quarter or more of positions closed, are communications; food service; motor transport; CBRN defense; ground ordnance maintenance; ground electronics maintenance; engineer, construction, facilities, and equipment; and Marine Air Ground Task Force (MAGTF) plans (see Table C.2 in Appendix C for details).

The type and magnitude of gender restrictions based on unit closures differs by rank group. Marine Corps officer specialties with closed positions due to direct ground combat unit missions include

- 0202 intelligence (89 percent open)
- 0402 logistics (83 percent open)
- 0180 adjutant (81 percent open)
- 1302 combat engineer (76 percent open).

Female warrant officers in the Marine Corps face relatively fewer limitations than their officer counterparts. In most occupations, 85 percent or more of positions are open to them. The two most heavily restricted occupations are the 2120 weapons repair officer (52 percent open) and the 5702 CBRN defense officer (54 percent open).

There are many enlisted MOSs with some closed positions. Enlisted specialties with 93 percent or more of their billets open to women are as follows:

- 0111 administrative Marine (94 percent open)
- 0481 landing support specialist (99 percent open)

- 1169 utilities chief (96 percent open)
- 1349 engineer equipment chief (95 percent open)
- 3052 packaging specialist (99.5 percent open)
- 4421 legal services (99.8 percent open)
- 5811 military police (100 percent open).

Overall, the 3531 motor vehicle operator MOS is the largest occupation with restrictions: There are 7,598 authorized positions, 76 percent of which are open to women. Because of the nature of that work (motor transport of supplies and personnel), female Marines in that MOS can find themselves temporarily attached to the ground combat units to which they cannot be permanently assigned.

The 2887 artillery electronics technician MOS has 95 percent of its 76 positions open to women, but no female Marines were assigned as of December 2010. No women held the 2891 electronics maintenance chief positions either, although 86 percent of those 122 authorized positions had no gender restrictions.

In addition to the magnitude of position closures in a given occupation, it is also important to understand whether the closed positions are important for career advancement or have an impact on job satisfaction and women's interest in remaining in the military. We explored this in greater detail for the communications career field.

Marine Corps Communications

The communications career field is the second largest career field in the Marine Corps (infantry is the largest), and it has the largest number of closed positions. Considering all ranks combined, 68 percent of the 14,007 authorized positions in communications are open to women. The career field manager reported that, for promotion, the Marine Corps considers whether Marines are performing well to support the warfighter, regardless of the position they hold.

For officers, 11 percent of the 723 authorized positions in the 0602 communications officer occupation are closed to women. The closed positions are located in low-altitude air defense in the air wing and below division in tank, infantry, combat engineer, combat assault, reconnaissance, and amphibious assault vehicle units.

As was the case with Army military intelligence officers, the higher pay grades have fewer formal gender restrictions. For 0602, the number of open positions drops by 5 percent for women advancing to the level of captain, but then jumps by 12 percent at major and opens completely at the level of lieutenant colonel:

- 88 percent of first lieutenant (O2) positions
- 83 percent of captain (O3) positions
- 95 percent of major (O4) positions
- 100 percent of lieutenant colonel (O5) positions.

Nearly all positions that can be filled by warrant officer communicators are open to women. Some enlisted occupations also have no restrictions: 0613 construction wireman (installation of cable and telephone wires), 0623 tropospheric scatter radio multichannel equipment operator, 0627 satellite communications operator-maintainer, and 0689 computer defense specialist.

But some enlisted specialties in communications do have restrictions:

- 0612 tactical switching operator (66 percent open)
- 0619 wire chief (76 percent open)
- 0621 field radio operator (46 percent open)
- 0622 digital (multichannel) wideband transmission equipment operator (88 percent open)
- 0629 radio chief (72 percent open)
- 0651 data systems technician (76 percent open)
- 0659 tactical data network gateway systems administrator (97 percent open)
- 0681 information security technician (90 percent open)
- 0699 communications chief (82 percent open).

According to the career field manager we interviewed, Marines can move across the communications MOSs, opening up opportunities that would not exist if they were confined completely to the duties in the MOS in which they entered. Through on-the-job training and experience with different communication technologies, Marines tend to drift toward the occupations for which they have an affinity and talent and can change MOSs after their first term.

If given a choice with limited unit manning, a commander will forgo many of the communication specialties, but the 0621 field radio operator is the most important to the operation of a unit. The career field manager explained that 0621 field radio operator positions are more likely to lead to the communications chief position, the senior MOS of all communicators. The following assignment opportunities in 0621 are open to women below the pay grade of E-6:

- 94 percent of private first class (E2) positions
- 51 percent of lance corporal (E3) positions
- 47 percent of corporal (E4) positions
- 55 percent of sergeant (E5) positions.

Among 0629 radio chief positions, however, there is more room to integrate women:

- 70 percent of staff sergeant (E6) positions
- 76 percent of gunnery sergeant (E7) positions.

Among the 0699 communications chief positions, the following are open to women:

- 80 percent of master sergeant (E8) positions
- 90 percent of master gunnery sergeant (E9) positions.

Although assignment opportunities widen for female Marines who become staff sergeants, the representation of women declines at the higher enlisted ranks. Women account for 11 percent of field radio operators but only 6 percent of the radio chiefs and 2 percent of communications chiefs (an MOS that also draws from the other communications MOSs). We do not have evidence to demonstrate whether that decline can be explained to any degree by limitations in early career assignments.

Communicators who serve in front-line combat units must be prepared to march, maneuver, and engage in direct ground combat, in addition to carrying out their communicator responsibilities. They do not simply travel with the infantry; they fill both the infantry role and the communicator role. The field radio operator is closest to supporting the infantryman, and the duty can be very difficult physically. A Marine in this position might deploy to Afghanistan with an infantry unit and have to carry supplies for the prescribed number of days in a backpack. Duties can involve patrolling while wearing prescribed loads, body armor, ammunition, and sustainment supplies; sleeping in snow; or patrolling in temperatures exceeding 100 degrees. The work can also be very satisfying through tasks such as calling in a medical evacuation to a save Marine lives or calling in aircraft or artillery strikes to support the unit.

Even communicators in other MOSs, or assigned to headquarters, may find themselves maneuvering with combat arms Marines, and they may need to fill in at the battalion level should a unit lose its assigned communicator to injury, illness, or death. Not all positions are mobile, however: As the career manager described, communicators cannot carry a switchboard around, and the satellite vehicle is attached to the command center, so satellite operator-maintainers are geographically stationary unless the command center relocates.

Overall, the size of this career field and the diversity of specialties afford women many channels through which to advance. The largest MOS, field radio operator, is also the one with the greatest gender restrictions. Assignment opportunities increase but women's representation decreases through the progression of the radio operator career. Across communications specialties, however, female Marines play an important role in today's operations in Iraq and Afghanistan. The career field manager contrasted today's gender integration in theater to that in the 1991 Gulf War, in which female Marines were confined to the air base while male Marines moved forward.

Conclusion

The largest occupations closed to female Marines fall in the infantry career field. Occupations in field artillery, tank and amphibious assault vehicles, and ground ordnance maintenance are among those closed to women. The Marine Corps recently opened two intelligence MOSs to women. For open occupations, positions below the division level in the ground combat element are closed. These restrictions affect a wide array of occupations to varying degrees for officers, warrant officers, and enlisted Marines. A closer look at the communicator positions highlights how opportunities for on-the-job training and movement to other communicator MOSs can provide enlisted women with assignment opportunities beyond what might be available in a single MOS. A greater percentage of communications officer positions are open to women than is the case in most enlisted MOSs in this field. However, the flexibility in enlisted assignments expands the range of possible positions beyond enlisted female communicators' current MOSs. In the largest and most constrained enlisted MOS, assignment opportunities increase once the rank of staff sergeant is reached, but women's representation also declines.

CHAPTER SEVEN

Navy Positions Closed to Women

Many of the Navy's closures are a result of berthing and privacy restrictions on ships and submarines. Additionally, positions on the Navy's riverine boat crews, in special warfare, and in Marine Corps ground combat elements are closed. Table A.4 in Appendix A and Tables B.8 and B.9 in Appendix B provide additional details on closed positions; Appendix D contains data about berthing availability on ships open to enlisted women (the assignment of officer women does not require berthing modifications). A spotlight on the field medical service technician specialty illustrates limitations on the assignment of female Sailors to Navy and Marine Corps units.

Positions Closed Due to Berthing and Privacy Restrictions

The Navy has been the primary service to employ the 1994 provision that positions may be closed to women "where the Service Secretary attests that the costs of appropriate berthing or privacy arrangements are prohibitive." The berthing and privacy issue is shaped by the configuration of many Navy seagoing vessels and the conditions that naval personnel experience when afloat on sea duty while assigned to a ship. Naval personnel may spend months living on a ship, sharing close quarters and a limited number of restroom facilities. Under these conditions, the number of military personnel is managed to ensure that men and women have separate living quarters and restrooms and that pay grade and occupational requirements for the ship are also met.

As officer quarters afford a higher degree of privacy than those of enlisted personnel, most vessels are open to female officers regardless of whether modifications have been made. On large ships, some percentage of "rack space" is allocated for enlisted women. Although the number of women on a given ship may be relatively constant over time, the occupations held by these women may not be.

Ships

Several types of ships remain closed to enlisted women due to berthing limitations. All enlisted billets on patrol craft and missile-guided frigates are closed. The closure of patrol craft (other than riverine craft)[1] and frigates closes 424 and 4,040 positions to women, respectively. Restrictions on these types of vessels affect positions in a diverse set of ratings, including BM boatswain's mate, EN engineman, GM gunner's mate, IT information systems, ET electronics technician, FC fire control, LS logistics specialist, and CS culinary specialist.

Among the types of ships open to women, most do have some facilities designated for enlisted women (see Appendix D). Many but not all of the older ships have accommodations for women. For example, 16 of the 22 guided missile cruisers can accommodate enlisted women. Of those, 10–12 percent of junior enlisted racks and 10–20 percent of chief petty officer racks are typically designated for women. As of December 2010, Navy women accounted for 16 percent of personnel in those junior pay grades and 8 percent of chief petty officers. Thus, most guided missile cruisers open to women do not have enough space to accommodate the proportion of enlisted women in the Navy, nor do they have sufficient space to compensate for the lack of racks for women on all-male guided missile cruisers. All 11 aircraft carriers contain berthing for enlisted women. Yet, the available space on five of them is at or below the percentage of junior enlisted women in the Navy. Still, because women are disproportionately represented in occupations that have many shore-based assignments (e.g., legal, yeoman, hospital corpsman), the ship spaces reserved for women are often filled below capacity. Berthing space for female chief petty officers is also below their representation among chief petty officers, although slightly less so. Appendix D offers additional details on the available rack space on ships, by type of naval vessel open to women. To ensure the Navy's ability to achieve the optimal mix of skill, experience, and rank on each ship and to provide the appropriate rotation of sea and shore assignments for both women and men, the Navy WISR representatives reported that the Navy is updating its shipboard habitability design criteria and practices. The representatives indicated that the new requirements will specify that future modifications to Navy vessels will provide modular berthing and restroom facilities that are gender-neutral and thus can accommodate any ratio of men to women. Improvements to shipboard habitability would benefit not only women but men as well: A 1999 Navy quality-of-life survey found that "shipboard living is a serious dissatisfier for Sailors at all ranks, especially the structural limitations of heads [restrooms], privacy and berthing" (Naval Research Advisory Committee, 2001, p. 71).

Overhauls of old ships and the construction of new ones have already facilitated an increase in the number of ships with space open to enlisted and officer women. A 1994 memo to the Secretary of Defense, for example, reported that all afloat staffs, all combat air squadrons, aircraft carriers, cruisers, destroyers, frigates,[2] amphibious war-

---

[1] Closed due to the direct ground combat mission of those boat crews, not berthing or privacy limitations.

[2] Although frigates are open to women, none has been reconfigured to provide berthing space for enlisted women.

fare ships, mine countermeasure commands and mine countermeasure support ships, and all units of the Naval Construction Force would open to women. Although the decommissioning of noncombatant ships actually caused the number of berths for women to decline in the mid-1990s, the modification of combatant ships helped those numbers begin to recover (Ebbert and Hall, 1999 p. 332). In 1999, the Navy opened mine countermeasure and mine coastal hunter ships classes to women. In 2005, coastal patrol craft ships were open to female officers. Today, more positions closed to women are located on submarines than on ships.

Submarines

Restrictions also affect assignment to submarines, where space is even more limited than it is on ships. A total of 13,000 closed positions are on submarines or require submarine-related occupations or experience. Until recently, berthing limitations closed all submarine positions to women. In 2010, the Navy significantly expanded opportunities for women by opening officer careers on ballistic missile and guided missile submarines, as well as positions on those submarines for officer women in other career fields. Only the smaller fast-attack submarines are still off-limits to female officers due to berthing configuration, which equates to 845 authorized positions, 20 of which are for limited-duty officers (LDOs).[3] Once guided missile submarines joined the fleet, the Navy determined that between those positions and positions on ballistic missile submarines, female officers would have sufficient opportunities to pursue the diversity of assignments and leadership roles needed to reach command without having to serve on fast-attack submarines. Consequently, the Navy opened this career path to them. This advance is a milestone for Navy women.

All enlisted positions on submarines remain closed to women, however. On many submarines, personnel must pass through enlisted sleeping quarters to access work areas, limiting privacy for Sailors. The Navy reports that there are currently no plans to modify submarine berthing during routine maintenance to accommodate both men and women. In a letter dated December 1, 2010, however, the Secretary of Defense notified Congress of the Navy's intention to expend funds to reconfigure existing submarines to accommodate female crew members, starting with design and study efforts.

A total of 12,128 submarine positions are closed to enlisted women. Specifically, policy closes the following submarine-specific ratings (enlisted occupations) to women: two of the ET electronic technician specialties (ETN electronic technician navigator and ETR electronic technician radio), FT fire control technician, one IT specialty (ITS information systems technician), two MM machinists mate specialties (MME machinists mate auxiliary and MMW machinists mate weapons), MT missile tech-

---

[3] LDOs are the officer technical managers of their staff or line corps and advance to positions of leadership within their former enlisted ratings. These leadership and management positions are at the ensign through captain levels and require technical background and skills not attainable through the typical officer designators.

nician, and the STS submarine sonar technician rating. Women in non–submarine-specific ratings, such as YN yeoman, CS culinary specialist, and LS logistics specialist, are unable to fill submarine assignments. For example, 280 positions (5 percent of positions) in the yeomen rating and 659 culinary specialist positions (9 percent of all culinary specialist positions) are closed to women because they are located on submarines. Submarine restrictions also close at least 70 job specialties (NECs), including acoustic intelligence technician, combat control system operator, submarine nuclear propulsion plant operator, and minesweeping electrician.[4]

In addition to enlisted closures, there are also warrant officer and LDO submarine-related positions that are closed to women on these large submarines. However, Navy policy states that these restrictions are not due to berthing constraints but exist because women cannot acquire the prerequisite enlisted experience on submarines to qualify for these jobs. Closed submarine LDO positions are in the designators 6210 deck, 6230 engineering/repair, 6260 ordnance, 6280 electronics, and 6290 communications. Closed submarine warrant officer specialties are in the 7210 boatswain/deck, 7230 engineering, 7240 repair, 7260 ordnance, 7280 electronics, and 7400 nuclear power. If any enlisted positions on submarines were to open, these positions would also open but could take some time to fill as women move up the enlisted ranks on submarines. However, there are already exceptions to the rule. Navy representatives reported that, as of June 2011, three women have been designated 6260 LDO ordnance (a closed specialty) and were accepted into the submarine community, although they are detailed to weapon facilities ashore rather than onboard submarines. Although the majority of closures are related directly or indirectly to berthing and privacy limitations, there are other types of restrictions as well.

Other Navy Closures: Riverine and Special Warfare

In 2007, the newly created Riverine Group 1's Riverine Squadron 1 deployed to Iraq, representing the Navy's first use of a riverine force since the Vietnam War (Hamilton, 2007). All officer and enlisted positions assigned to riverine boat crews are closed to women, but because of the direct ground combat mission not because of berthing and privacy concerns. Female officers may fill some positions in riverine squadrons, but they are not permitted to lead boat crews. This closure affects 18 out of 3,747 unrestricted line officer surface warfare positions. The 351 enlisted riverine boat crew positions that are closed span the ratings of BM boatswain's mate, ET electronics technician, GM gunner's mate, and CT cryptologic technician. These restrictions are new since the 1994 policy; the Navy's riverine force did not exist at the time.

---

[4] NECs relate to ratings but may correspond to more than one. Ratings, not NECs, are shown in the appendix tables.

Additional positions closed to women are located in the Naval Special Warfare Command, which includes sea-air-land (SEAL) units and special boat teams. SEAL teams conduct land, sea, and underwater operations and are highly skilled combat swimmers; each team consists of about 108 personnel, 12 of them officers (Feickert, 2011). In the special warfare officer community, there is one closed unrestricted line officer career field (designator 113X) with 653 positions in the June 2011 authorization data, along with one closed LDO designator (615X) with 49 positions. As a part of the WISR review, the SEAL detailer identified 32 unrestricted line officer positions currently requiring the closed 1130 special warfare officer designator that could potentially be filled by other unrestricted line officers, pending approval of the gaining command. These positions are all nonoperational and shore-based, including titles such as regional strategist, exercise planner, assessment officer, maritime operations planner, force structure officer, international engagement officer, and SEAL/Naval special warfare project manager.

The two chief warrant officer (CWO) specialties in special warfare are also closed to women.[5] The special warfare technician CWO (715X) has 66 authorized positions, and the special warfare combatant craft technician (717X) has 33 positions. The two enlisted ratings closed to women are SO special warfare operator (2,059 positions) and SB special warfare boat operator (785 positions).

The Navy has sought ways to expand assignment opportunities to women across communities. For example, there are shore-based health care positions with the Navy SEALs that do not require combat deployment with those units and therefore are open to both genders. Because the Navy does not code its authorizations by gender, there has been confusion about whether women can serve in units such as these.

Navy Positions in Marine Corps Units

Marine Corps unit closures have implications for gender restrictions in some Navy positions, including hospital corpsman, religious program specialists, chaplain, medical officer, and naval gunfire liaison officer (NGLO). Navy women serving in support of the Fleet Marine Force are assigned in accordance with Marine Corps policy, meaning that they are prohibited from serving in direct ground combat units.

The Navy provides all medical and religious services personnel for Marine Corps units. The Navy reported that, as of July 2011, 77 medical officers (designator 2100), 70 chaplains (officer designator 4100), and 307 religious program specialists (enlisted rating RP) occupied closed positions in Marine Corps infantry regiments and at bat-

[5] CWO positions are for technical specialists, but CWOs may also serve as division officers, department heads, officers in charge, executive officers, and commanding officers, ashore or afloat. Navy CWOs are considered commissioned officers and have the authority, experience, and knowledge to direct challenging operations within a given occupational specialty.

talion level and below in tank, artillery, combat assault, combat engineer, amphibious assault, force reconnaissance, and light armored reconnaissance units. Only 2 percent of medical officer positions are closed, however. For chaplains, just 8 percent of positions are closed, compared to 41 percent of religious program specialist positions. Enlisted women fill 26 percent of religious program positions, so assignment limitations may be more apparent to them than to the 7 percent of chaplains who are women.

Field Medical Service Technicians

The largest occupation assigned to Marine Corps units and affected by ground combat–related closures draws from the Navy's HM hospital corpsman enlisted rating. There are 23,254 authorized positions for Sailors in the hospital corpsman career path. These health care providers can become field medical service technicians (NEC 8404) by completing Marine Corps training in the skills necessary to manage combat trauma casualties and to maneuver with Marine Corps forces in a combat environment. Although this field medical service technician specialty was created to meet Marine Corps needs, the Navy also values this additional combat training among its hospital corpsman and employs them in its Naval Special Warfare Command and Navy Expeditionary Combat Command. This specialty also has the distinction of having some positions designated to be filled with women, because, as described by a career field manager, the units want to ensure that there is a female health care provider to help meet the needs of the female population.

A Navy hospital corpsman career field manager reported that, overall, there are authorizations for 8,951 field medical service technicians, with 56 percent of positions closed to women, 5 percent of positions closed to men, and the remainder available to either men or women. Table 7.1 breaks those numbers out by Navy and Marine Corps positions, showing that nearly all of the male-only positions are in the Marine Corps.

After 8404 field medical service technician specialty training, wider assignment opportunities are available to hospital corpsmen: In addition to Navy hospitals, ships, and clinics, they may serve tours with Marine Corps units. Given the limited flexibility in assigning women, the Marine Corps needs the majority of the corpsmen it trains to be men so that they can meet the greatest need in the ground combat units, especially if casualties run high. A very small number of male 8404 field medical service tech-

Table 7.1
Gender Restrictions on NEC 8404 Field Medical Service Technicians

Service	Male Only	Female Only	No Gender Restriction
Marine Corps	4,941	426	313
Navy	32	7	3,232
Total positions	4,973	433	3,545

nicians undergo additional training to serve in Marine Corps reconnaissance units. There are currently 125 men serving in these positions.

The Navy career field managers reported that although female hospital corpsmen who wish to serve in "front-line" ground combat units do not have the opportunity to do so, these closed assignments are not critical for advancement to the senior enlisted ranks. Moreover, because the need for 8404s has persisted over the course of the wars in Iraq and Afghanistan, and because there are often not enough volunteers to serve in Marine Corps units or to deploy to the current theaters of operation, the career field managers have ample opportunities to find placement outside of direct ground combat units for any women who would volunteer to become 8404s.

Looking more broadly at the HM hospital corpsman rating, however, when we consider the sum of the limitations that ban women from serving in Marine Corps units and on Navy riverine boat teams, patrol craft, submarines, and frigates, we find that 77 percent of authorized positions are available to women, who make up 20 percent of the rating. We do not have visibility from the authorization data about which positions are more likely to be filled, if not all authorized positions can be filled due to personnel or funding shortages. If shortages are managed by filling all types of positions relatively equally, then the percentage of positions open to women may be unaffected. If positions closed to women in ground combat units or on vessels such as submarines take priority, then the percentage of positions open to women will shrink. Alternatively, if positions in hospitals, clinics, or ships that are open to women take priority, then a greater percentage of positions will be open.

Naval Gunfire Liaison Officers

Naval gunfire liaison officers advise force commanders on naval gunfire support, plan and direct gunfire support, and carry out duties to accomplish those objectives. Some NGLOs are located at the division level for planning purposes rather than field execution. NGLO is not a career field but a type of assignment that the authorizations data indicate can be filled by surface warfare and aviation officers, surface warfare LDOs, or warrant officers. There are 45 NGLO positions assigned to Marine Corps units. These positions account for less than 1 percent of positions for the two officer occupations (111X and 1300), 5 percent of the LDO positions, and 10 percent of warrant officer positions.

There is some ambiguity surrounding the NGLO positions. Navy policy lists the positions as closed due to collocation with direct ground combat units, which would mean they would open to women if the collocation restriction were lifted. The Marine Corps, however, considers these positions direct ground combat and listed air-naval gunfire liaison companies as closed in 1994 due to direct ground combat, which was reaffirmed by the Marine Corps WISR representatives. Regardless, in Table B.8 in Appendix B, we counted these 45 positions as closed to women. However, there appear to be some exceptions. The NGLO placement officer noted that, because the authorization data do not indicate any gender restrictions, a few women (four, as of August 2011) have been assigned to NGLO positions. Other Navy representatives noted that women in those positions do not serve in direct ground combat roles, that there are officers in NGLO positions who are not serving in NGLO roles, and that there are officers outside of NGLO positions serving in NGLO roles, so there is some flexibility in how NGLO requirements are met by surface warfare personnel. Because of the gender restrictions, however, female NGLOs can fill fewer roles than their male counterparts.

Conclusion

Based on the Navy's policy, clarification from Navy representatives, and our tabulations of the authorization data, we found that the majority of positions closed due to berthing and privacy constraints are located on submarines (13,000 closed positions) rather than frigates or patrol craft (4,464 closed positions). The first female Navy officers trained to serve on submarines are expected to graduate in the fall of 2011. Submarine-related LDO and warrant officer positions are not open to women because women cannot obtain the prerequisite enlisted experience on submarines. To provide privacy for enlisted men and women on submarines, modification of existing berthing is necessary.

To provide greater flexibility in meeting the Navy's needs and to better sustain women's career opportunities for sea duty, the revised Navy policy requires future ship modifications to include gender-neutral modular designs.

Not all positions in Navy units are closed due to limited accommodations. Navy women are also prohibited from serving in the 369 authorized positions on the newly established riverine boat crews because of their direct ground combat missions, although other riverine positions are open to them. Occupations devoted to special warfare are closed to women and account for a total of 3,645 positions.

Some Navy positions in Marine Corps units are closed to women, but the impact is less significant on chaplain and medical officers than on the female enlisted Sailors in the RP religious program and HM hospital corpsman ratings. The field medical service technician training provides some combat skills training and qualifies hospital corpsmen to serve in Marine Corps units as well as Navy units, but just over half of those positions are closed. When the field medical service technician closures are combined with other closures on Navy riverine boat crews, frigates, patrol craft, and submarines, a total of 23 percent of the 23,254 assignments are closed to women. This gives the Navy less flexibility in assigning the 20 percent of the rating who are women, but given the size of this occupation, the Navy has much more flexibility than it does in the smaller occupations. NGLO positions are officially closed to female officers, LDOs, and warrant officers in the surface warfare community, but a few women do serve in them, although not in direct ground combat roles.

CHAPTER EIGHT

Conclusions and Recommendations

In support of the WISR, DoD requested that RAND describe—relative to gender restriction policies—the military occupations that are closed to women and the occupations that are open but have some positions that are closed. We were also asked to quantify the closed positions for the active components of each service.

Across DoD active components in fiscal year 2011, 252,695 authorized positions, or 21 percent, of 1,220,118 are closed to military women.[1] All closed occupations in the Air Force are special operations occupations and equate to less than 1 percent of Air Force positions. Air Force personnel assigned to Army units follow the Army's assignment policy, but very few of those positions have been closed to women because the positions have not been located below the brigade level. Tabulations from the service authorization data indicate that the majority of positions in occupations that are closed to women fall under the Army and Marine Corps infantry, armored vehicle, and field artillery career fields. All positions in the infantry and armor career fields are closed to women, and most field artillery positions in the Army are closed and all field artillery positions in the Marine Corps. Although these positions constitute only three career fields in each of these services, they encompass a majority of closed positions.

These closed combat arms occupations are among the most physically challenging occupations in the Army and Marine Corps, but they are also at the core of the ground forces' mission. As such, they produce many of the two services' most senior leaders.

That men in occupations open to women can fill a wider array of types of assignments raises the question of whether they are more likely to obtain the breadth and type of assignments needed for personnel to be considered competitive for promotion in their career field. We did not analyze men's and women's career paths, however. Men also have to disproportionately fill some of the most physically challenging roles while serving in direct ground combat units—roles that may involve greater exposure to austere living conditions, heavy lifting and foot patrols, hostile fire, and risk of injury or death.

---

[1] This count of authorized positions excludes spaces reserved for patients, prisoners, students, trainees, and personnel in transition.

Our interviews with career field managers suggested that some particularly large career fields or career fields with few gender restrictions may offer sufficient assignment opportunities to permit women to be highly competitive as well. Furthermore, specialties in great demand during wartime may offer excellent promotion opportunities regardless of the types of assignments that men and women can fill, particularly for those who excel in their duties.

In the Navy, we found that the majority of positions closed due to berthing and privacy constraints are on submarines rather than frigates or patrol craft. Occupations in special warfare are closed, as are submarine-specific LDO, warrant officer, and enlisted occupations. Women cannot fill LDO and warrant officer positions on submarines only because they cannot acquire the prerequisite enlisted experience on submarines. Some Sailors serve in Marine Corps units: Female Sailors face the same types of constraints on service in the ground combat element that female Marines do.

In military occupations open to women but with some positions closed, both policy and our analyses of the authorization data show that the closures are located primarily in the smaller direct ground combat units and thus have a more significant impact on the availability of jobs at the junior officer level. Further along the career path, at higher levels in the organization, opportunities for women widen. A study of individual careers would be necessary to determine whether the closures have a negative impact on women's career paths. Such a study should take service members' career preferences into account and not assume that most desired the career path is the one that moves personnel up the ranks the fastest or is the most prestigious. Personnel may have differing preferences for particular work environments (e.g., office, field, work pace), deployment cycles, geographic stability, duty hours/compatibility with family life, financial benefits (e.g., from serving in a combat zone), diversity of work assignments, and so forth.

Recommendations for Improved Recordkeeping

Over the course of this research effort, we discovered instances of ambiguity, errors, and conflicting information about whether positions were closed to women. Thus, we recommend that the services improve the tracking, accuracy, and visibility of positions that are closed to military women. All the services should code as such any positions closed to women in the authorization databases. "Closed positions" should include positions that women cannot fill, whether because of the type of unit, the required occupation or additional skills, lack of berthing and privacy accommodations, or other reasons. Without coding closures based on prerequisites or required occupations needed to fill positions, the data would provide an incomplete picture. Thus, such an approach would provide visibility to DoD and service leadership about which positions are closed and also eliminate the need to rely solely on detailers, career field managers, and requesting/receiving commanders to fully understand and consistently apply the exclusion policies, which may be open to differing interpretations.

The services should also undertake a periodic review of closures to permit timely updates in light of relevant changes, such as technological developments affecting the physical demands of certain jobs, the redefinition or creation of military specialties, or advances in the way in which forces are organized or operate on the battlefield.

APPENDIX A

Military Occupations Closed to Women

The tables in this appendix list the military occupations that are completely closed to women in the Air Force, Army, Marine Corps, and Navy. This information was compiled as part of the WISR initiative. For officers, warrant officers, and enlisted personnel, the tables contain the occupational codes and titles identified as closed to women by the service representatives in the WISR working group. Corresponding occupational/career field information was obtained from service occupational guides. As an indication of the size of the occupation, the tables also indicate the number of active-component authorized positions for fiscal year 2011.

Table A.1
Air Force Occupations Closed to Women

Rank Group	Occupational Code	Title	Occupational/Career Field	Total Authorizations
Officer	13DXA	Combat Rescue Officer	Space, Missile, Command and Control	128
	13DXB	Special Tactics Officer	Space, Missile, Command and Control	86
Enlisted	1C2X1	Combat Controller	Command and Control Systems Operations	521
	1C4X1	Tactical Air Control Party (TACP)	Command and Control Systems Operations	1,721
	1T2X1	Pararescue	Aircrew Protection	581
	1W0X2	Special Operations Weather	Weather	111

SOURCE: Data on the total number of authorizations are from the MPW, March 2011.

Table A.2
Army Occupations Closed to Women

Rank Group	Occupational Code	Title	Occupational/Career Field	Total Authorizations
Officer	11A	Infantry	Infantry	3,744
	18A	Special Forces	Special Forces	1,057
	19A	Armor, General	Armor	385
	19B	Armor	Armor	505
	19C	Cavalry	Armor	895
Warrant	180A	Special Forces Warrant Officer	Special Forces	567
Enlisted	11B	Infantryman	Infantry	50,518
	11C	Indirect Fire Infantry	Infantry	5,591
	11Z	Infantry Senior Sergeant	Infantry	1,741
	12B	Combat Engineer	Engineering	10,158
	13B	Cannon Crewmember	Field Artillery	9,470
	13C	Tactical Automated Fire Control Systems	Field Artillery	0
	13D	Field Artillery Automated Tactical Data System Specialist	Field Artillery	3,188
	13E	Cannon Fire Direction Specialist	Field Artillery	0
	13F	Fire Support Specialist	Field Artillery	5,958
	13M	Multiple Launch Rocket System (MLRS/HIMARS) Crewmember	Field Artillery	1,746
Enlisted	13P	Multiple Launch Rocket System Operations/Fire Direction Specialist	Field Artillery	897
	13R	Field Artillery Firefinder Radar Operator	Field Artillery	673

Table A.2—Continued

Rank Group	Occupational Code	Title	Occupational/Career Field	Total Authorizations
Enlisted (cont.)	18B	Special Forces Weapons Sergeant	Special Forces	1,168
	18C	Special Forces Engineer Sergeant	Special Forces	1,035
	18D	Special Forces Medical Sergeant	Special Forces	858
	18E	Special Forces Communications Sergeant	Special Forces	1,130
	18F	Special Forces Assistant Operations and Intelligence Sergeant	Special Forces	501
	18Z	Special Forces Senior Sergeant	Special Forces	1,166
	19D	Cavalry Scout	Armor	10,641
	19K	M1 Armor Crewman	Armor	6,652
	19Z	Armor Senior Sergeant	Armor	658
	91A	M1 Abrams Tank System Maintainer	Mechanical Maintenance	1,114
	91M	Bradley Fighting Vehicle System Maintainer	Mechanical Maintenance	1,531
	91P	Artillery Mechanic	Mechanical Maintenance	432

SOURCE: Data on the total number of authorizations are from the PMAD database, March 2011.

Table A.3
Marine Corps Occupations Closed to Women

Rank Group	Occupational Code	Title	Occupational/Career Field	Total Authorizations
Officer	0203	Ground Intelligence Officer	Intelligence	151
	0302	Infantry Officer	Infantry	1,587
	0802	Field Artillery Officer	Field Artillery	639
	0840	Naval Surface Fire Support Planner	Field Artillery	1
	1802	Tank Officer	Tank and Assault Amphibious Vehicle	111
	1803	Assault Amphibious Vehicle Officer	Tank and Assault Amphibious Vehicle	107
	7204	Low Altitude Air Defense Officer	Air Control/Air Support/ Anti-Air Warfare/Air Traffic Control	32
	7502[a]	Forward Air Controller	Pilots/Naval Flight Officers	165
Warrant	0306	Infantry Weapons Officer	Infantry	105
	0803	Targeting Acquisition Officer	Field Artillery	30
	2110	Ordnance Maintenance Vehicle Officer	Ground Ordnance Maintenance	49
Enlisted	0311	Rifleman	Infantry	14,416
	0313	Light Armored Vehicle Crewman	Infantry	934
	0321	Reconnaissance Man	Infantry	1,428
	0331	Machine Gunner	Infantry	2,702
	0341	Mortarman	Infantry	2,775
	0351	Infantry Assaultman	Infantry	1,179

Table A.3—Continued

Rank Group	Occupational Code	Title	Occupational/Career Field	Total Authorizations
Enlisted (cont.)	0352	Antitank Missileman	Infantry	1,340
	0369	Infantry Unit Leader	Infantry	2,054
	0811	Field Artillery Cannoneer	Field Artillery	2,241
	0814	High Mobility Artillery Rocket System (HIMARS) Operator	Field Artillery	0
	0842	Field Artillery Radar Operator	Field Artillery	243
	0844	Field Artillery Fire Control Man	Field Artillery	583
	0847	Artillery Meteorological Man	Field Artillery	125
	0848	Field Artillery Operations Man	Field Artillery	221
	0861	Fire Support Man	Field Artillery	586
	1812	M1A1 Tank Crewman	Tank and Assault Amphibious Vehicle	675
	1833	Assault Amphibious Vehicle Crewman	Tank and Assault Amphibious Vehicle	1,992
	1834	Expeditionary Fighting Vehicle (EFV) Crewman	Tank and Assault Amphibious Vehicle	1
	2131	Towed Artillery Systems Technician	Ground Ordnance Maintenance	201
	2141	Assault Amphibious Vehicle Repairer/Technician	Ground Ordnance Maintenance	719
	2146	Main Battle Tank Repairer/Technician	Ground Ordnance Maintenance	409
	2147	Light Armored Vehicle Repairer/Technician	Ground Ordnance Maintenance	446
	2149	Ordnance Vehicle Maintenance Chief	Ground Ordnance Maintenance	52

Table A.3—Continued

Rank Group	Occupational Code	Title	Occupational/Career Field	Total Authorizations
Enlisted (cont.)	7212	Low Altitude Air Defense Gunner	Air Control/Air Support/Anti-Air Warfare/Air Traffic Control	356
	8152[a]	Marine Corps Security Force Guard	Miscellaneous Requirement MOS	233
	8154[a]	Marine Corps Security Force Close Quarters Battle Team Member	Miscellaneous Requirement MOS	20

SOURCE: Data on the total number of authorizations are from TFSMS, January 2011.

[a] 7502 and 8154 are free MOSs and can be filled by Marines with any PMOS. 8152 is an exception MOS that can be filled by an enlisted Marine holding PMOS 0311, 0331, 0351, 0369, or 5811.

Table A.4
Navy Occupations Closed to Women

Rank Group	Occupational Code	Title	Occupational/ Career Field	Total Authorizations
Officer	113X	Special Warfare Unrestricted Line Officer (Underwater Demolition Team/SEAL Officer)	Special Warfare	653
	615X	Special Warfare Limited Duty Officer	Special Warfare	49
	6210	Limited Duty Officer, Deck	Undersea Warfare	9
	6230	Limited Duty Officer, Engineering/Repair	Undersea Warfare	36
	6260[a]	Limited Duty Officer, Ordnance	Undersea Warfare	119
	6280	Limited Duty Officer, Electronics	Undersea Warfare	69
	6290	Limited Duty Officer, Communications	Undersea Warfare	56
Warrant	715X	Special Warfare Technician Chief Warrant Officer	Special Warfare	66
	717X	Special Warfare Combatant Craft Technician Chief Warrant Officer	Special Warfare	33
	7210	Warrant Officer, Boatswain/Deck	Undersea Warfare	3
	7230	Warrant Officer, Engineering Technician	Undersea Warfare	6
	7240	Warrant Officer, Repair Technician	Undersea Warfare	0
	7260	Warrant Officer, Ordnance Technician	Undersea Warfare	16
	7280	Warrant Officer, Electronics Technician	Undersea Warfare	6
	7400	Warrant Officer, Nuclear Power Technician	General	45
Enlisted	FT	Fire Control Technician (Submarine)	Weapons Control	1,138
	MT	Missile Technician (Submarine)	Ordnance Systems	1,057

Table A.3—Continued

Rank Group	Occupational Code	Title	Occupational/ Career Field	Total Authorizations
Enlisted (cont.)	SB	Special Warfare Boat Operator	Special Warfare/Diving	785
	SO	Special Warfare Operator (Underwater Demolition Team/SEAL)	Special Warfare/Diving	2,059
	STS	Sonar Technician, Submarine	Sensor Operations	2,023

SOURCE: Data on the total number of authorizations are from TFMMS, June 2011.

[a] The Navy reports that, as of June 2011, three women were designated 6260 and were accepted into the submarine community, although they are detailed to weapon facilities ashore rather than aboard submarines.

APPENDIX B

Open Military Occupations with Positions Closed to Women

Tables B.1 through B.9 list the open military occupations that include positions that are closed to women in the Air Force, Army, Marine Corps, and Navy. For officers, warrant officers, and enlisted personnel, each table contains the occupational codes and titles identified as having positions closed to women by the service representatives in the WISR working group. Corresponding occupational/career field information was obtained from service occupational guides. The tables also provide the percentage and number of positions closed to women in each occupation according to authorization data provided by each service. Finally, the tables display the percentage of active-component personnel in each occupation who are women, based on data in the December 2010 Defense Manpower Data Center DEERS PITE personnel files.

It is important to note that, for the Marine Corps, Tables B.5, B.6, and B.7 list only PMOSs unless a specialty has no specific PMOS linked to it, in which case the specialty is marked with a note in the table. The MOS listed is generally the first (entry-level) job in a series, but the data for the entire series are included in that entry. This reflects Marine Corps practices as well. For example, PMOS 0602 communications is listed as an open MOS with some closed positions. The 0603 C4 planner position, a more advanced position that requires additional training, is linked to 0602, and the data for both are reflected in the 0602 row. Other assignments or necessary MOSs may have certain PMOS prerequisites.[1]

[1] A necessary MOS is a non-PMOS that has a prerequisite of one or more PMOSs. This specialty identifies a particular skill or training that supplements the Marine's PMOS, but only Marines with a specific PMOS can attain it.

Table B.1
Air Force Occupations with Some Positions Closed to Women

Rank Group	Occupational Code	Title	Occupational/ Career Field	Location of Closed Positions	Total Authorizations	Percentage of Positions Open to Women	Percentage of Positions Filled by Women
Officer	11XXU	Pilot: Air Liaison Officer	Operations	Army infantry battalions[a]	279	100	4.9
Officer	12XXU	Combat System Officer: Air Liaison Officer	Operations	Army infantry battalions[a]	81	100	2.2
Officer	13LX	Air Liaison Officer	Space, Missile, Command and Control	Army infantry battalions[a]	26	100	0.0
Officer	15W	Weather	Operations	Army special operations units	507	97.2	20.8
Officer	18AXU	Remotely Piloted Aircraft: Air Liaison Officer	Operations	Army infantry battalions[a]	0	NA	No positions
Enlisted	3D1X3	Radio Frequency Transmission Systems	Cyberspace Support	Army infantry/special operations forces battalions[b]	3,365	97.9	8.1

SOURCES: Information on restrictions provided by Air Force WISR representatives. Data on the total number of authorizations and the percentage of positions open to women are from the MPW, March 2011. Data on the percentage of positions filled by women are from DEERS PITE personnel files, December 2010.

[a] ALOs have not been serving at the battalion level, but any ALO positions assigned to that level by the Army would be closed to women.

[b] 3D1X3 radio frequency transmission systems has had closures based on the expectation that these Airmen would be assigned to Army infantry battalions. Because they have been serving in Army brigades instead, and thus have not been collocated or involved in direct ground combat, these positions are likely to open to women.

Table B.2
Army Officer Occupations with Some Positions Closed to Women

Occupational Code	Title	Occupational/ Career Field	Location of Closed Positions	Total Authorizations	Percentage of Positions Open to Women	Percentage of Positions Filled by Women
00B	General Officer	Branch Immaterial	Commanding general positions in active Army divisions and corps	390	90.8	5.3
01A	Officer Generalist	Branch Immaterial	Ranger battalions and headquarters and headquarters battalions of divisions	3,743	99.2	14.8
02A	Combat Arms Generalist	Combat Arms Immaterial	Maneuver battalions, anti-armor companies, reconnaissance squadrons, ranger battalions, long-range surveillance, special forces battalions, engineer companies in brigade combat teams, mobility augmentation companies, sapper companies, special operations aviation battalions, cannon battalions (field artillery), and some Iraq- and Afghanistan-coded units	3,492	77.8	6.3
02B	Infantry/Armor Immaterial	Combat Arms Immaterial	Maneuver battalions, anti-armor companies, reconnaissance squadrons, ranger battalions, long-range surveillance, and special forces battalions	587	6.1	0.2
02C	Infantry/Armor/Field Artillery/Engineer Immaterial	Combat Arms Immaterial	Maneuver battalions, anti-armor companies, reconnaissance squadrons, ranger battalions, long-range surveillance, special forces battalions, engineer companies in brigade combat teams, mobility augmentation companies, sapper companies, and cannon battalions (field artillery)	112	0.9	0.0
12A	Engineer, General	Engineer	Maneuver battalions and some Iraq- and Afghanistan-coded positions	414	99.0	10.2

Table B.2—Continued

Occupational Code	Title	Occupational/ Career Field	Location of Closed Positions	Total Authorizations	Percentage of Positions Open to Women	Percentage of Positions Filled by Women
12B	Combat Engineer	Engineer	Maneuver battalions, reconnaissance squadrons, engineer companies in brigade combat teams, mobility augmentation companies, sapper companies, headquarters and ranger regiments, special troops battalions, sustainment brigades, and some training units	1,540	73.2	11.0
12D	Facilities/Contract Construction Management Engineer (FCCME)	Engineer	1 special forces battalion and 1 unit with no description	461	99.8	8.0
13A	Field Artillery, General	Field Artillery	Maneuver battalions, reconnaissance squadrons, ranger battalions, cannon battalions (field artillery)	3,264	33.1	1.0
14A	Air Defense Artillery Officer	Air Defense Artillery	1st Squadron, 11th Armored Cavalry Regiment, and Headquarters and Headquarters Company, 172nd Infantry Brigade	1,038	99.3	11.3
15A	Aviation, General	Aviation	Special operations aviation battalions	495	99.4	9.9
15B	Aviation Combined Arms Operations	Aviation	Special operations aviation battalions	1,867	90.8	8.0
25A	Signal, General	Signal Corps	Maneuver battalions, reconnaissance squadrons, ranger battalions, special forces battalions, cannon battalions (field artillery), and some Iraq- and Afghanistan-coded units	2,643	89.4	17.7
27A	Judge Advocate General	Judge Advocate General	Special forces battalions and ranger battalions	1,573	98.6	25.0

Table B.2—Continued

Occupational Code	Title	Occupational/ Career Field	Location of Closed Positions	Total Authorizations	Percentage of Positions Open to Women	Percentage of Positions Filled by Women
29A	Electronic Warfare Officer	Electronic Warfare	Ranger battalions and 172nd Infantry Brigade	61	96.6	0.0
30A	Information Operations Officer	Information Operations	Ranger battalions	379	99.7	6.3
31A	Military Police	Military Police	Maneuver battalions and Iraq-coded units	1,426	97.4	19.6
35D	All Source Intelligence	Military Intelligence	Maneuver battalions, reconnaissance squadrons, ranger battalions, special forces battalions, cannon battalions, and Iraq- and Afghanistan-coded units	2,738	86.1	20.3
35E	Counterintelligence	Military Intelligence	Ranger battalions	307	99.7	14.3
36A	Financial Manager	Financial Management	Special operations aviation battalions and at regiment level in 75th Ranger Regiment and 160th Special Operations Aviation Regiment	580	99.0	23.7
37A	Psychological Operations	Psychological Operations	1 special operations unit	375	99.7	13.9
38A	Civil Affairs	Civil Affairs	Special forces battalions and ranger battalions	547	92.7	10.2
42B	Human Resources Officer	Adjutant General	Maneuver battalions, reconnaissance squadrons, ranger battalions, special forces battalions, special operations aviation battalions, cannon battalions (field artillery), and some Iraq- and Afghanistan-coded units	1,138	80.1	44.8
42H	Senior Human Resources Officer	Adjutant General	Special forces battalions, ranger battalions, special operations aviation battalions, and Afghanistan-coded units	771	99.2	31.1

Table B.2—Continued

Occupational Code	Title	Occupational/ Career Field	Location of Closed Positions	Total Authorizations	Percentage of Positions Open to Women	Percentage of Positions Filled by Women
50A	Force Development	Force Development	1 special operations unit	207	99.5	8.9
51A	Systems Development	Acquisition	Office of the Program Manager, Saudi Arabian National Guard Modernization Program, and 2 special operations units	435	98.6	8.8
51C	Contract and Industrial Management	Acquisition	1 unit with no description	354	99.7	12.0
51R	Systems Automation Acquisition and Engineering	Acquisition	1 special operations unit	73	97.3	14.0
51T	Test and Evaluation	Acquisition	1 special operations unit	55	98.6	8.3
51Z	Acquisition	Acquisition	Office of the Program Manager, Saudi Arabian National Guard Modernization Program, and 2 special operations units	690	99.3	8.9
53A	Information Systems Management	Information Systems Management	Ranger battalions and Office of the Program Manager, Saudi Arabian National Guard Modernization Program	665	99.7	12.0
56A	Command and Unit Chaplain	Chaplain	Maneuver battalions, reconnaissance squadrons, ranger battalions, special forces battalions, special operations aviation battalions, cannon battalions (field artillery)	1,515	99.7	3.9
57A	Simulations Operations Officer	Simulations Operations	Ranger battalions and reconnaissance squadrons	263	98.9	4.5
59A	Strategist	Strategic Plans and Policy	1 special operations unit	333	99.7	8.3

Table B.2—Continued

Occupational Code	Title	Occupational/ Career Field	Location of Closed Positions	Total Authorizations	Percentage of Positions Open to Women	Percentage of Positions Filled by Women
60A	Operational Medicine	Medical Corps	Office of the Program Manager, Saudi Arabian National Guard Modernization Program	164	99.4	18.6
62B	Field Surgeon	Medical Corps	Maneuver battalions, reconnaissance squadrons, ranger battalions, special forces battalions, special operations aviation battalions, cannon battalions (field artillery)	201	85.1	21.4
65B	Physical Therapy	Medical Specialist Corps	Ranger battalions	206	98.5	37.2
65D	Physician Assistant	Medical Specialist Corps	Maneuver battalions, reconnaissance squadrons, ranger battalions, special forces battalions, special operations aviation battalions, cannon battalions (field artillery)	809	71.0	22.4
70B	Health Services Administration	Health Services	Maneuver battalions, reconnaissance squadrons, ranger battalions, special force battalions, special operations aviation battalions, cannon battalions (field artillery)	550	62.7	30.8
70H	Health Services Plans, Operations, Intelligence, Security and Training	Health Services	Office of the Program Manager, Saudi Arabian National Guard Modernization Program, and ranger battalions	468	99.1	19.6
70K	Health Services Materiel	Health Services	Office of the Program Manager, Saudi Arabian National Guard Modernization Program	386	99.8	24.1
73B	Clinical Psychology	Behavioral Sciences	Special operations aviation battalions and 1 special troops battalion	131	98.5	43.2

Table B.2—Continued

Occupational Code	Title	Occupational/ Career Field	Location of Closed Positions	Total Authorizations	Percentage of Positions Open to Women	Percentage of Positions Filled by Women
74A	Chemical, Biological, Radiological, and Nuclear (CBRN)	Chemical Corps	Maneuver battalions, anti-armor companies, reconnaissance squadrons, ranger battalions, special forces battalions, and cannon battalions (field artillery)	1,017	78.9	26.2
88A	Transportation, General	Transportation Corps	Ranger battalions and some Iraq- and Afghanistan-coded units	903	99.7	20.9
90A	Logistics	Logistics	Ranger battalions, special forces battalions, special operations aviation battalions, and some Iraq-coded units	2,697	97.6	17.8
91A	Maintenance and Munitions Materiel Officer	Ordnance	Reconnaissance squadrons; mobility acquisition companies; some Iraq- and Afghanistan-coded units; Office of the Program Manager, Saudi Arabian National Guard Modernization Program; support battalions; and some Army medical detachments	1,320	99.8	15.3
92A	Quartermaster, General	Quartermaster Corps	Maneuver battalions, reconnaissance squadrons, ranger battalions, special forces battalions, special operations aviation battalions, and cannon battalions (field artillery)	1,244	99.3	48.0

SOURCES: Data on the total number of authorizations and the percentage of positions open to women are from the PMAD database, March 2011. Data on the percentage of positions filled by women are from DEERS PITE personnel files, December 2010.

NOTE: Information about the location of closed positions is based on PMAD header and detail files, March 2011.

Table B.3
Army Warrant Officer Occupations with Some Positions Closed to Women

Occupational Code	Title	Occupational/ Career Field	Location of Closed Positions	Total Authorizations	Percentage of Positions Open to Women	Percentage of Positions Filled by Women
011A	Branch/MOS Immaterial	NA	1 unit with no unit description	59	96.6	13.0
120A	Construction Engineering Technician	Engineer	Headquarters and headquarters battalions of I and III Corps	129	98.4	0.0
131A	Field Artillery Targeting Technician	Field Artillery	Cannon battalions (field artillery) and fires brigades	379	65.2	0.6
140A	Command and Control Systems Integrator	Air Defense Artillery	525th and 504th Battlefield Surveillance Brigades	136	98.5	4.6
150U	Unmanned Aircraft Systems Operations Technician	Aviation	Reconnaissance squadrons	179	92.2	5.8
151A	Aviation Maintenance Technician (Nonrated)	Aviation	Office of the Program Manager, Saudi Arabian National Guard Modernization Program, and special operations aviation battalions	213	93.0	8.2
153D	UH-60 Pilot	Aviation	Special operations aviation battalions and 1 Iraq-coded unit	1,632	99.8	3.6
153E	MH-60 Pilot	Aviation	Special operations aviation battalions and at the regiment level in the 160th Special Operations Aviation Regiment	203	0.0	0.0
154C	CH-47D Pilot	Aviation	Special operations aviation battalions	173	97.1	2.0
154E	MH-47 Pilot	Aviation	Special operations aviation battalions and at the regiment level in the 160th Special Operations Aviation Regiment	150	0.0	0.0

Table B.3—Continued

Occupational Code	Title	Occupational/ Career Field	Location of Closed Positions	Total Authorizations	Percentage of Positions Open to Women	Percentage of Positions Filled by Women
155A	Fixed Wing Aviator (Aircraft Nonspecific)	Aviation	1 special operations unit	59	98.3	2.3
251A	Information Systems Technician	Signal Corps	Ranger battalions, special operations aviation battalions, and 1 unit with no unit description	304	99.0	23.6
254A	Signal Systems Support Technician	Signal Corps	Ranger battalions, special forces battalions, and special operations aviation battalions	219	86.8	11.4
290A	Electronic Warfare Technician	Electronic Warfare	Ranger battalions, fires brigades, and 172nd Infantry Brigade	57	78.9	12.5
350F	All Source Intelligence Technician	Military Intelligence	Reconnaissance squadrons, ranger battalions, long-range surveillance, and special operations aviation battalions	429	96.3	9.5
351L	Counter-Intelligence Technician	Military Intelligence	Ranger battalions and special operations aviation battalions	333	99.4	9.5
351M	Human Intelligence Collection Technician	Military Intelligence	1 special troops battalion	244	99.6	10.5
352P	Voice Intercept Technician	Military Intelligence	1 special troops battalion	40	97.5	6.4
420A	Human Resources Technician	Adjutant General's Corps	Headquarters and headquarters company ranger regiment	346	99.7	38.4
740A	Chemical, Biological, Radiological, and Nuclear (CBRN) Warrant Officer	Chemical Corps	Cannon battalions (field artillery)	12	66.7	Missing in assignment data
882A	Mobility Officer	Transportation Corps	1 special troops battalion	167	99.4	22.1

Table B.3—Continued

Occupational Code	Title	Occupational/ Career Field	Location of Closed Positions	Total Authorizations	Percentage of Positions Open to Women	Percentage of Positions Filled by Women
890A	Ammunition Technician	Ordnance	Special operations aviation battalions, 1 unknown special forces unit, and 1 special troops battalion	157	98.1	19.2
915A	Automotive Maintenance Warrant Officer	Ordnance	Maneuver battalions, reconnaissance squadrons, ranger battalions, special forces battalions, special operations aviation battalions, cannon battalions (field artillery)	651	94.6	5.1
919A	Engineer Equipment Maintenance Warrant Officer	Ordnance	Engineer companies in brigade combat teams	138	98.6	3.8
920A	Property Accounting Technician	Quartermaster Corps	Special forces battalions and cannon battalions (field artillery)	431	90.0	38.8
920B	Supply Systems Technician	Quartermaster Corps	1 special troops battalion	263	99.6	41.5
921A	Airdrop Systems Technician	Quartermaster Corps	Ranger battalions, special forces battalions, and 1 special troops battalion	79	91.1	8.2
948B	Electronic Systems Maintenance Warrant Officer	Electronic Maintenance	Special operations aviation battalions	182	97.8	7.7

SOURCES: Data on the total number of authorizations and the percentage of positions open to women are from the PMAD database, March 2011. Data on the percentage of positions filled by women are from DEERS PITE personnel files, December 2010.

NOTE: Information about the location of closed positions is based on PMAD header and detail files, March 2011.

Table B.4
Army Enlisted Occupations with Some Positions Closed to Women

Occupational Code	Title	Occupational/ Career Field	Location of Closed Positions	Total Authorizations	Percentage of Positions Open to Women	Percentage of Positions Filled by Women
00D	Special Duty Assignment	Personnel Special Reporting Code	Headquarters of divisions and corps	331	87.3	9.5
00Z	Command Sergeant Major	Personnel Special Reporting Code (Sergeant Major)	Maneuver battalions, reconnaissance squadrons, ranger battalions, special forces battalions, special operations aviation battalions, and cannon battalions (field artillery)	1,382	76.8	5.7
12C	Bridge Crewmember	Combat Engineering	Engineer companies in brigade combat teams, mobility augmentation companies, and sapper companies	800	93.0	16.2
12D	Diver	Combat Engineering	Special forces battalions	153	99.3	2.0
12N	Horizontal Construction Engineer	Combat Engineering	Engineer companies in brigade combat teams, mobility augmentation companies, and sapper companies	3,668	89.5	4.7
12R	Interior Electrician	Combat Engineering	Ranger battalions	418	98.6	7.2
12W	Carpentry and Masonry Specialist	Combat Engineering	Ranger battalions	809	99.3	8.0
12Y	Geospatial Engineer	Combat Engineering	Maneuver battalions, long-range surveillance, engineer companies in brigade combat teams, mobility augmentation companies, and sapper companies	1,021	97.8	22.5
12Z	Combat Engineering Senior Sergeant	Combat Engineering	Engineer companies in brigade combat teams, mobility augmentation companies, and sapper companies	291	68.0	0.9

Table B.4—Continued

Occupational Code	Title	Occupational/ Career Field	Location of Closed Positions	Total Authorizations	Percentage of Positions Open to Women	Percentage of Positions Filled by Women
13T	Field Artillery Surveyor/ Meteorological Crewmember	Artillery	Cannon battalions (field artillery) and fires brigades	651	12.0	10.9
13Z	Field Artillery Senior Sergeant	Artillery	Cannon battalions (field artillery), fires brigades, and battlefield coordination detachments	722	46.5	0.5
14J	Air Defense Command, Control, Communications, Computers and Intelligence Tactical Operations Center Enhanced Operator/ Maintainer	Air Defense	Battlefield coordination detachments	1,931	98.9	8.3
14S	Air and Missile Defense (AMD) Crewmember	Air Defense	Brigade-level headquarters and headquarters companies	900	89.0	6.7
14Z	Air Defense Artillery Senior Sergeant	Air Defense	1 closed position, 4th Squadron, 11th Armored Cavalry Regiment	241	99.6	3.9
15B	Aircraft Powerplant Repairer	Aviation	Special forces battalions and special operations aviation battalions	571	88.8	2.0
15D	Aircraft Powerplant Repairer	Aviation	Special operations aviation battalions	492	87.4	5.1
15E	Unmanned Aircraft System	Aviation	Reconnaissance squadrons, ranger battalions, special forces battalions, and special operations aviation battalions	378	87.0	12.3
15F	Aircraft Electrician	Aviation	Special operations aviation battalions	425	85.6	3.7

Table B.4—Continued

Occupational Code	Title	Occupational/ Career Field	Location of Closed Positions	Total Authorizations	Percentage of Positions Open to Women	Percentage of Positions Filled by Women
15G	Aircraft Structural Repairer	Aviation	Special operations aviation battalions	616	83.3	3.4
15H	Aircraft Pneudraulics Repairer	Aviation	Special operations aviation battalions	435	92.2	3.6
25B	Information Technology Specialist	Signal Corps	Maneuver battalions, reconnaissance squadrons, ranger battalions, long-range surveillance, special forces battalions, special operations aviation battalions, cannon battalions (field artillery), and fires brigades	7,298	90.5	18.5
25C	Radio Operator-Maintainer	Signal Corps	Maneuver battalions, reconnaissance squadrons, ranger battalions, long-range surveillance, special forces battalions, special operations aviation battalions, cannon battalions (field artillery), and some Iraq-coded units	870	70.6	6.5
25E	Electromagnetic Spectrum Manager	Signal Corps	Maneuver battalions, reconnaissance squadrons, and ranger battalions	243	97.5	6.8
25F	Network Switching Systems Operator-Maintainer	Signal Corps	Special forces battalions	878	95.9	9.8
25L	Cable Systems Installer-Maintainer	Signal Corps	1 cannon battalion (field artillery)	1,549	99.7	17.9
25N	Nodal Network Systems Operator-Maintainer	Signal Corps	1 special troops battalion	1,221	99.5	8.1
25P	Microwave Systems Operator-Maintainer	Signal Corps	Special forces battalions and ranger battalions	718	93.7	9.8

Table B.4—Continued

Occupational Code	Title	Occupational/ Career Field	Location of Closed Positions	Total Authorizations	Percentage of Positions Open to Women	Percentage of Positions Filled by Women
25Q	Multichannel Transmission Systems Operator-Maintainer	Signal Corps	Maneuver battalions, reconnaissance squadrons, cannon battalions (field artillery)	3,544	89.8	12.3
25S	Satellite Communications Systems Operator-Maintainer	Signal Corps	Special forces battalions	2,949	95.8	4.8
25T	Satellite/Microwave Systems Chief	Signal Corps	2 units with no unit description	105	97.1	7.2
25U	Signal Support Systems Specialist	Signal Corps	Maneuver battalions, reconnaissance squadrons, ranger battalions, long-range surveillance, special forces battalions, sapper companies, special operations aviation battalions, cannon battalions (field artillery), and fires brigades	8,002	62.7	14.6
25W	Telecommunications Operations Chief	Signal Corps	Special forces battalions and Iraq-coded units	1,121	95.5	11.1
25Z	Visual Information Operations Chief	Signal Corps	2 units with no unit description	114	96.5	16.0
27D	Paralegal Specialist	Judge Advocate General	Maneuver battalions, reconnaissance squadrons, ranger battalions, special forces battalions, special operations aviation battalions, and cannon battalions (field artillery)	1,552	84.4	36.2
29E	Electronic Warfare Specialist	Electronic Warfare	Maneuver battalions, reconnaissance squadrons, special forces battalions, special operations aviation battalions, cannon battalions (field artillery), and fires brigades	264	43.6	7.0

Table B.4—Continued

Occupational Code	Title	Occupational/ Career Field	Location of Closed Positions	Total Authorizations	Percentage of Positions Open to Women	Percentage of Positions Filled by Women
31B	Military Police	Military Police Corps	8th Military Police Brigade headquarters and headquarters company	14,922	99.9 (1 closed position)	13.3
35F	Intelligence Analyst	Military Intelligence	Maneuver battalions, reconnaissance squadrons, ranger battalions, long-range surveillance, special forces battalions, special operations aviation battalions, cannon battalions (field artillery), and some Iraq- and Afghanistan-coded units	6,158	74.2	19.0
35G	Imagery Analyst	Military Intelligence	Reconnaissance squadrons, special forces battalions, and special operations aviation battalions	1,589	96.3	14.0
35L	Counter Intelligence Agent	Military Intelligence	Special forces battalions, special operations aviation battalions, and 1 special troops battalion	1,183	94.3	15.5
35M	Human Intelligence Collector	Military Intelligence	Special forces battalions	2,972	89.2	20.3
35N	Signals Intelligence Analyst	Military Intelligence	Special forces battalions and special operations aviation battalions	2,934	96.2	16.4
35P	Cryptologic Linguist	Military Intelligence	Special forces battalions	2,289	85.6	22.1
35T	Military Intelligence (MI) Systems Maintainer/ Integrator	Military Intelligence	Special forces battalions	786	97.7	6.2
35X	Intelligence Senior Sergeant/Chief Intelligence Sergeant	Military Intelligence	Special forces battalions, special operations aviation battalions, and some Iraq-coded units	294	91.8	9.9

Table B.4—Continued

Occupational Code	Title	Occupational/ Career Field	Location of Closed Positions	Total Authorizations	Percentage of Positions Open to Women	Percentage of Positions Filled by Women
35Z	Signals Intelligence (SIGINT) Senior Sergeant/SIGINT Chief	Military Intelligence	Reconnaissance squadrons	288	97.2	9.0
36B	Financial Management Technician	Finance Corps	Ranger battalions and special operations aviation battalions	1,635	99.0	35.2
37F	Psychological Operations Specialist	Psychological Operations	9th Psychological Operations Battalion	1,012	77.5	10.7
38B	Civil Affairs Specialist	Civil Affairs	Civil affairs brigades and JFK Special Warfare School	499	92.2	4.0
42A	Human Resources Specialist	Adjutant General	Maneuver battalions, reconnaissance squadrons, ranger battalions, special forces battalions, special operations aviation battalions, cannon battalions (field artillery), and some Iraq- and Afghanistan-coded units	11,568	84.4	43.3
46Q	Public Affairs Specialist	Public Affairs	172nd nfantry Brigade headquarters and headquarters company	325	99.4	34.9
46R	Public Affairs Broadcast Specialist	Public Affairs	172nd nfantry Brigade headquarters and headquarters company	293	99.7	32.1
56M	Chaplain Assistant	Chaplain's Corps	Maneuver battalions, reconnaissance squadrons, special forces battalions, special operations aviation battalions, and cannon battalions (field artillery)	1,501	84.1	26.7
68J	Medical Logistics Specialist	Medical	Ranger battalions	1,146	99.7	39.4
68S	Preventive Medicine Specialist	Medical	Special forces battalions	595	96.6	37.0

Table B.4—Continued

Occupational Code	Title	Occupational/ Career Field	Location of Closed Positions	Total Authorizations	Percentage of Positions Open to Women	Percentage of Positions Filled by Women
68W	Health Care Specialist	Medical	Maneuver battalions, anti-armor companies, reconnaissance squadrons, ranger battalions, long-range surveillance, special forces battalions, engineer companies in brigade combat teams, mobility augmentation companies, sapper companies, special operations aviation battalions, cannon battalions (field artillery), and some Iraq-coded units	19,562	65.8	22.9
68X	Behavioral Health Specialist	Medical	1 special troops battalion	739	99.9	38.5
74D	Chemical, Biological, Radiological, and Nuclear (CBRN) Specialist	Chemical Warfare	Maneuver battalions, anti-armor companies, reconnaissance squadrons, ranger battalions, long-range surveillance, special forces battalions, engineer companies in brigade combat teams, mobility augmentation companies, sapper companies, special operations aviation battalions, cannon battalions (field artillery), and some Iraq- and Afghanistan-coded units	6,954	79.7	23.1
79S	Career Counselor	Recruiting and Retention	Ranger battalions	1,005	99.6	24.6
88M	Motor Transport Operator	Transportation	Maneuver battalions, anti-armor companies, reconnaissance squadrons, ranger battalions, long-range surveillance, special forces battalions, engineer companies in brigade combat teams, mobility augmentation companies, sapper companies, special operations aviation battalions, cannon battalions (field artillery), and some Iraq-coded units	16,625	98.5	14.7

Table B.4—Continued

Occupational Code	Title	Occupational/ Career Field	Location of Closed Positions	Total Authorizations	Percentage of Positions Open to Women	Percentage of Positions Filled by Women
88N	Transportation Management Coordinator	Transportation	Reconnaissance squadrons, ranger battalions, special forces battalions, and special operations aviation battalions	2,226	97.6	22.5
88Z	Transportation Senior Sergeant	Transportation	Some Iraq-coded units	259	99.6	13.3
89B	Ammunition Specialist	Explosives and Ammunition	Special forces battalions and special operations aviation battalions	2,569	96.1	21.8
89D	Explosive Ordnance Disposal Specialist	Explosives and Ammunition	Office of the Program Manager, Saudi Arabian National Guard Modernization Program	2,067	100.0	4.4
91B	Wheeled Vehicle Repairer	Maintenance	Maneuver battalions, anti-armor companies, reconnaissance squadrons, special forces battalions, engineer companies in brigade combat teams, mobility augmentation companies, sapper companies, cannon battalions (field artillery), and some Iraq-coded units	15,948	96.1	5.8
91C	Utilities Equipment Repairer	Maintenance	Special operations aviation battalions	1,403	99.1	7.2
91D	Power Generation Equipment Repairer	Maintenance	Maneuver battalions, reconnaissance squadrons, ranger battalions, special forces battalions, and cannon battalions (field artillery)	3,124	96.1	9.9
91E	Allied Trades Specialist	Maintenance	Reconnaissance squadrons, ranger battalions, special forces battalions, special operations aviation battalions, and cannon battalions (field artillery)	1,225	95.8	7.2
91F	Small Arms/Artillery Repairer	Maintenance	Special forces battalions and special troops battalions	944	96.7	16.0

Table B.4—Continued

Occupational Code	Title	Occupational/ Career Field	Location of Closed Positions	Total Authorizations	Percentage of Positions Open to Women	Percentage of Positions Filled by Women
91G	Fire Control Repairer	Maintenance	Ranger battalions and support battalions	287	95.8	22.6
91H	Tracked Vehicle Repairer	Maintenance	Maneuver battalions, reconnaissance squadrons, engineer companies in brigade combat teams, mobility augmentation companies, sapper companies, cannon battalions (field artillery), and special troops battalions	1,855	83.7	6.9
91J	Quartermaster and Chemical Equipment Repairer	Maintenance	Maneuver battalions, reconnaissance squadrons, special forces battalions, engineer companies in brigade combat teams, mobility augmentation companies, and special operations aviation battalions	1,307	94.8	17.6
91K	Armament Repairer	Maintenance	Ranger battalions and 1 Iraq-coded unit	582	99.5	9.8
91L	Construction Equipment Repairer	Maintenance	Ranger battalions, engineer companies in brigade combat teams, and special troops battalions	1,203	23.0	10.0
91X	Maintenance Supervisor	Maintenance	Maneuver battalions, reconnaissance squadrons, ranger battalions, special forces battalions, engineer companies in brigade combat teams, mobility augmentation companies, sapper companies, and special operations aviation battalions	2,236	96.8	6.3
91Z	Senior Maintenance Supervisor	Maintenance	Maneuver battalions, reconnaissance squadrons, engineer companies in brigade combat teams, and cannon battalions (field artillery)	815	94.1	4.6

Table B.4—Continued

Occupational Code	Title	Occupational/ Career Field	Location of Closed Positions	Total Authorizations	Percentage of Positions Open to Women	Percentage of Positions Filled by Women
92A	Automated Logistical Specialist	Supply and Logistics	Maneuver battalions, reconnaissance squadrons, ranger battalions, long-range surveillance, special forces battalions, engineer companies in brigade combat teams, mobility augmentation companies, sapper companies, special operations aviation battalions, and cannon battalions (field artillery)	10,766	96.7	40.0
92F	Petroleum Supply Specialist	Supply and Logistics	Maneuver battalions, reconnaissance squadrons, ranger battalions, special forces battalions, engineer companies in brigade combat teams, mobility augmentation companies, special operations aviation battalions, and cannon battalions (field artillery)	9,398	95.5	14.6
92G	Food Service Specialist	Supply and Logistics	Maneuver battalions, reconnaissance squadrons, ranger battalions, special forces battalions, engineer companies in brigade combat teams, mobility augmentation companies, and cannon battalions (field artillery)	9,804	94.9	26.9
92L	Petroleum Laboratory Specialist	Supply and Logistics	Ranger battalions	194	98.5	27.6
92R	Parachute Rigger	Supply and Logistics	Ranger battalions, special forces battalions, and special operations aviation battalions	1,515	84.4	11.8
92S	Shower/Laundry and Clothing Repair Specialist	Supply and Logistics	1 unit with no unit description	946	99.7	27.1
92W	Water Treatment Specialist	Supply and Logistics	Special forces battalions	1,953	98.5	23.2

Table B.4—Continued

Occupational Code	Title	Occupational/ Career Field	Location of Closed Positions	Total Authorizations	Percentage of Positions Open to Women	Percentage of Positions Filled by Women
92Y	Unit Supply Specialist	Supply and Logistics	Maneuver battalions, anti-armor companies, reconnaissance squadrons, ranger battalions, long-range surveillance, special forces battalions, engineer companies in brigade combat teams, mobility augmentation companies, sapper companies, special operations aviation battalions, cannon battalions (field artillery), and some Iraq-coded units	12,178	72.0	34.2
94E	Radio and Communications Security (COMSEC) Repairer	Electronic/ Missile Maintenance	Ranger battalions, special forces battalions, and special operations aviation battalions	1,275	95.6	9.6
94M	Radar Repairer	Electronic/ Missile Maintenance	Cannon battalions (field artillery)	250	57.2	3.9
94R	Avionic and Survivability Equipment Repairer	Electronic/ Missile Maintenance	Special operations aviation battalions	360	92.8	11.0
94W	Electronic Maintenance Chief	Electronic/ Missile Maintenance	Special forces battalions and special operations aviation battalions	305	91.1	12.0
94Z	Senior Electronic Maintenance Chief	Electronic/ Missile Maintenance	1 unit with no unit description	90	98.9	4.1

SOURCES: Data on the total number of authorizations and the percentage of positions open to women are from the PMAD database, March 2011. Data on the percentage of positions filled by women are from DEERS PITE personnel files, December 2010.

NOTE: Information about the location of closed positions is based on PMAD header and detail files, March 2011.

Table B.5
Marine Corps Officer Occupations with Some Positions Closed to Women

Occupational Code	Title	Occupational/ Career Field	Location of Closed Positions	Total Authorizations	Percentage of Positions Open to Women	Percentage of Positions Filled by Women
0180	Adjutant	Personnel and Administration	Headquarters and service company in light armored reconnaissance, amphibious assault vehicle, reconnaissance, tank, infantry, and combat engineer battalions; headquarters battery in artillery battalion	310	81.2	32.4
0202	Marine Air/Ground Task Force (MAGTF) Intelligence Officer	Intelligence	Headquarters and service company in light armored reconnaissance, amphibious assault vehicle, reconnaissance, tank, infantry, and combat engineer battalions; and force reconnaissance company in reconnaissance battalion	585	89.4	4.1
0402	Logistics Officer	Logistics	Headquarters and service company in light armored reconnaissance, amphibious assault vehicle, reconnaissance, tank, infantry, combat assault, and combat engineer battalions; amphibious assault vehicle company in amphibious assault vehicle battalion; engineer support company in combat engineer battalion; and headquarters battery in artillery battalion	1,108	83.3	12.0
0530 (FMOS)	Civil Affairs Officer	Marine Air Ground Task Force (MAGTF) Plans	Headquarters battery and company in infantry regiments	50	84.0	6.3
0602	Communications Officer	Communications	Headquarters and service company in light armored reconnaissance battalion, amphibious assault vehicle, reconnaissance, tank, infantry, combat assault, and combat engineer battalions; headquarters battery in artillery battalion and low-altitude air defense battalion	723	88.9	7.4

Table B.5—Continued

Occupational Code	Title	Occupational/ Career Field	Location of Closed Positions	Total Authorizations	Percentage of Positions Open to Women	Percentage of Positions Filled by Women
1302	Combat Engineer Officer	Engineer, Construction, Facilities, and Equipment	Combat engineer company, engineer support company, and headquarters and service company in combat engineer battalion	376	76.1	7.7
2102	Ordnance Officer	Ground Ordnance Maintenance	Headquarters and service company in combat assault battalion	40	97.5	0.0
3002	Ground Supply Officer	Food Supply Administration and Operations	Headquarters and service company in light armored reconnaissance, amphibious assault vehicle, reconnaissance, tank, infantry, combat assault, and combat engineer battalions; amphibious assault vehicle company in amphibious assault vehicle battalion; and headquarters battery in artillery battalion and low-altitude air defense battalion	461	83.5	11.0
7202	Air Command and Control Officer	Air Control/Air Support/Anti-Air Warfare/Air Traffic Control	Headquarters and service battery in low-altitude air defense battalion	152	93.4	6.7
7208	Air Support Control Officer	Air Control/Air Support/Anti-Air Warfare/Air Traffic Control	Headquarters and service battery in low-altitude air defense battalion	166	98.8	0.0
7506 (FMOS)	Billet Designator	Pilots/Naval Flight Officers	Headquarters battery and company in infantry regiments and when the required MOS is closed to women (7502)	362	97.7	5.2
8007 (FMOS)	Billet Designator	Miscellaneous Requirements	Headquarters and service company in reconnaissance battalion; combat assault company in infantry regiment; filled only by ground officers	372	98.9	2.0

Table B.5—Continued

Occupational Code	Title	Occupational/ Career Field	Location of Closed Positions	Total Authorizations	Percentage of Positions Open to Women	Percentage of Positions Filled by Women
8041 (PMOS)	Colonel, Ground	Miscellaneous Requirements	Headquarters battery and company in infantry regiments	284	96.1	3.9

SOURCES: Data on total authorizations are from TFSMS, January 2011. Marine Corps WISR representatives identified which positions are open to women. Data on the percentage of positions filled by women are from DEERS PITE personnel files, December 2010.

NOTE: All occupational codes are for PMOSs except where noted. A free MOS (FMOS) can be filled by any Marine regardless of PMOS; FMOSs are unrelated to PMOS skills. A billet is not restricted based on any particular FMOS. However, if that billet is located in a unit in which female assignments are restricted, then that billet will also be restricted. Closed positions listed in the table are located below the division level in the ground combat elements, except where otherwise noted.

Table B.6
Marine Corps Warrant Occupations with Some Positions Closed to Women

Occupational Code	Title	Occupational/ Career Field	Location of Closed Positions	Total Authorizations	Percentage of Positions Open to Women	Percentage of Positions Filled by Women
0430	Mobility Officer	Logistics	Infantry regiment	104	92.3	8.7
1120	Utilities Officer	Utilities	Engineer company in combat assault battalion; engineer support company in combat engineer battalion	44	90.9	6.7
1310	Engineer Equipment Officer	Engineer, Construction, Facilities, and Equipment	Combat engineer company in combat assault battalion; engineer support company in combat engineer battalion	72	94.4	0.0
2120	Weapons Repair Officer	Ground Ordnance Maintenance	Headquarters and service company in light armored reconnaissance, amphibious assault vehicle, and tank battalions; headquarters battery in artillery battalion and headquarters company in infantry regiment	52	51.9	4.5
2805	Data/Communications Maintenance Officer	Ground Electronics Maintenance	Headquarters and service company in light armored reconnaissance, amphibious assault vehicle, tank, and combat assault battalions	60	86.6	5.4
3510	Motor Transport Maintenance Officer	Motor Transport	Headquarters and service company in tank and combat assault battalions; engineer support company in combat engineering battalion; headquarters battery in artillery battalion	106	84.9	1.0
5702	Chemical, Biological, Radiological, and Nuclear Defense Officer	Chemical, Biological, Radiological, and Nuclear Defense	Headquarters and service company in light armored reconnaissance, amphibious assault vehicle, tank, infantry, combat assault, and combat engineer battalions; headquarters battery in artillery battalion	123	54.4	0.0

SOURCES: Data on total authorizations are from TFSMS, January 2011. Marine Corps WISR representatives identified which positions are open to women. Data on the percentage of positions filled by women are from DEERS PITE personnel files, December 2010.

NOTE: All occupational codes are for PMOSs. Closed positions listed in the table are located below the division level in the ground combat elements.

Table B.7
Marine Corps Enlisted Occupations with Some Positions Closed to Women

Occupational Code	Title	Occupational/ Career Field	Location of Closed Positions	Total Authorizations	Percentage of Positions Open to Women	Percentage of Positions Filled by Women
0111	Administrative Marine	Personnel and Administration	Headquarters and service company in light armored reconnaissance battalion, amphibious assault vehicle, reconnaissance, tank, infantry, and combat engineer battalions; headquarters battery in artillery battalion and low-altitude air defense battalion	6,133	93.6	23.1
0211	Counterintelligence/ HUMINT Specialist	Intelligence	Headquarters and service company in reconnaissance battalion	695	99.9	0.8
0231	Intelligence Specialist	Intelligence	Headquarters and service company in light armored reconnaissance, amphibious assault vehicle, reconnaissance, tank, infantry, and combat engineer battalions; headquarters battery in artillery battalion; force reconnaissance company in reconnaissance battalion and low-altitude air defense battalion	1,711	76.2	15.0
0411	Maintenance Management Specialist	Logistics	Headquarters and service company in light armored reconnaissance, amphibious assault vehicle, reconnaissance, tank, infantry, combat engineer, and combat assault battalions; amphibious assault vehicle company in amphibious assault vehicle battalion; artillery battery in artillery battalion; combat assault company in infantry regiment; engineer company in combat assault battalion; engineer support company in combat engineer battalion; light armored reconnaissance company in light armored reconnaissance battalion; rocket battery in artillery battalion; tank company in tank battalion; headquarters battery in artillery and battalion and low-altitude air defense battalion	969	71.7	17.0

Table B.7—Continued

Occupational Code	Title	Occupational/ Career Field	Location of Closed Positions	Total Authorizations	Percentage of Positions Open to Women	Percentage of Positions Filled by Women
0431	Logistics/ Embarkation Specialist	Logistics	Amphibious assault vehicle company in amphibious assault vehicle battalion; headquarters and service company in infantry battalion and low-altitude air defense battalion; headquarters battery in artillery battalion	1,123	86.6	12.0
0451	Airborne and Air Delivery Specialist	Logistics	Headquarters and service company, reconnaissance company in reconnaissance battalion	202	82.2	6.2
0481	Landing Support Specialist	Logistics	Headquarters and service company in light armored reconnaissance, amphibious assault vehicle, and combat assault battalions	900	99.3	7.2
0491	Logistics/Mobility Chief	Logistics	Headquarters and service company in tank, reconnaissance, and combat assault battalions; headquarters battery in artillery battalion	394	93.9	6.1
0511	MAGTF Planning Specialist	Marine Air Ground Task Force (MAGTF) Plans	Headquarters and service company in reconnaissance battalion; headquarters company in infantry regiment	286	93.4	9.7
0531 (FMOS)	Civil Affairs Noncommissioned Officer	Marine Air Ground Task force (MAGTF) Plans	Headquarters battery and company in infantry regiments	151	94.7	1.8
0612	Tactical Switching Operator	Communications	Headquarters and service company in light armored reconnaissance, amphibious assault vehicle, tank, infantry, combat engineer, and combat assault battalions; artillery battery in artillery battalion; headquarters battery in artillery battalion	1,811	65.6	12.8

Table B.7—Continued

Occupational Code	Title	Occupational/ Career Field	Location of Closed Positions	Total Authorizations	Percentage of Positions Open to Women	Percentage of Positions Filled by Women
0619	Wire Chief	Communications	Headquarters and service company in light armored reconnaissance, amphibious assault vehicle, tank, infantry, and combat assault battalions; headquarters battery in artillery battalion	283	75.6	6.7
0621	Field Radio Operator	Communications	Tank company in tank battalion; headquarters and service company, headquarters company in infantry regiment and in infantry battalion; rocket battery and force reconnaissance company in reconnaissance battalion; light armored reconnaissance company in light armored reconnaissance battalion; combat assault battalion; artillery battery in artillery battalion; headquarters battery in artillery battalion; amphibious assault vehicle company in amphibious assault vehicle battalion and low-altitude air defense battalion	4,957	45.5	10.7
0622	Digital (Multi-channel) Wideband Transmission Equipment Operator	Communications	Headquarters company in infantry regiment and battalion	543	88.2	8.7

Table B.7—Continued

Occupational Code	Title	Occupational/ Career Field	Location of Closed Positions	Total Authorizations	Percentage of Positions Open to Women	Percentage of Positions Filled by Women
0629	Radio Chief	Communications	Headquarters and service company in light armored reconnaissance, amphibious assault vehicle, reconnaissance, tank, infantry, combat engineer, and combat assault battalions; amphibious assault vehicle company in amphibious assault battalion; artillery battery in infantry battalion; combat assault company in infantry regiment; distant reconnaissance, force reconnaissance, and reconnaissance company in reconnaissance battalion; force reconnaissance company in reconnaissance battalion; rocket battery in infantry battalion; tank company in tank battalion; headquarters battery in artillery battalion and low-altitude air defense battalion	847	72.4	5.5
0651	Data Systems Technician	Communications	Headquarters and service company in light armored reconnaissance, amphibious assault vehicle, reconnaissance, tank, infantry, combat engineer, and combat assault battalions; rocket battery in artillery battalion; headquarters battery in artillery battalion and low-altitude air defense battalion	2,780	76.3	3.95
0659	Tactical Data Network Gateway Systems Administrator	Communications	Headquarters company in infantry regiment	503	96.8	4.2
0681	Information Security Technician	Communications	Headquarters and service company in light armored reconnaissance, amphibious assault vehicle, reconnaissance, tank, and combat engineer battalions; infantry regiment and headquarters battery in low-altitude air defense battalion	215	89.8	10.9

Table B.7—Continued

Occupational Code	Title	Occupational/ Career Field	Location of Closed Positions	Total Authorizations	Percentage of Positions Open to Women	Percentage of Positions Filled by Women
0699	Communications Chief	Communications	Headquarters and service company in light armored reconnaissance, amphibious assault vehicle, reconnaissance, tank, infantry, combat engineer, and combat assault battalions; headquarters battery in artillery battalion	332	82.2	2.0
1141	Electrician	Utilities	Headquarters and service company in light armored reconnaissance, tank, and combat assault battalions; engineer company in combat assault battalion; engineer support company in combat engineer battalion; detachment headquarters battery in artillery battalion	527	79.5	17.2
1142	Engineer Equipment Electrical Systems Technician	Utilities	Headquarters and service company in light armored reconnaissance, tank, and combat assault battalions; engineer company in combat assault battalion; engineer support company in combat engineer battalion; detachment headquarters battery in artillery battalion; headquarters battery in low-altitude air defense battalion and headquarters company in infantry regiment	802	90.0	5.5
1161	Refrigeration and Air Conditioning Technician	Utilities	Headquarters and service company in tank and combat assault battalions; headquarters battery and company in infantry regiment and low-altitude air defense battalion	377	96.0	1.6
1169	Utilities Chief	Utilities	Engineer company in combat assault battalion; engineer support company in combat engineer battalion	162	96.3	3.4

Table B.7—Continued

Occupational Code	Title	Occupational/ Career Field	Location of Closed Positions	Total Authorizations	Percentage of Positions Open to Women	Percentage of Positions Filled by Women
1171	Water Support	Utilities	Headquarters and service company in light armored reconnaissance and combat assault battalion; engineer company in combat assault battalion	626	97.6	8.1
1316	Metal Worker	Engineer, Construction, Facilities, and Equipment	Headquarters and service company in light armored reconnaissance, amphibious assault vehicle, tank, and combat assault battalions; amphibious assault company in amphibious assault vehicle battalion; combat assault company in infantry regiment; engineer company in combat assault battalion; engineer support company in combat engineer battalion; light armored reconnaissance company in light armored reconnaissance battalion; tank company in tank battalion	282	72.3	3.2
1341	Engineer Equipment Mechanic	Engineer, Construction, Facilities, and Equipment	Headquarters and service company in light armored reconnaissance, amphibious assault vehicle, reconnaissance, tank, and combat assault battalions; combat assault company in infantry regiment; combat engineer company in combat engineer battalion; engineer company in combat assault battalion; engineer support company in combat engineer battalion; detachment headquarters battery in artillery battalion	1,183	87.5	3.5
1345	Engineer Equipment Operator	Engineer, Construction, Facilities, and Equipment	Headquarters and service company in light armored reconnaissance, amphibious assault vehicle, tank, and combat assault battalions; combat assault company in infantry regiment; engineer company in combat assault battalion; engineer support company in combat engineer battalion; detachment headquarters battery in artillery battalion	1,462	88.1	1.2

Table B.7—Continued

Occupational Code	Title	Occupational/ Career Field	Location of Closed Positions	Total Authorizations	Percentage of Positions Open to Women	Percentage of Positions Filled by Women
1349	Engineer Equipment Chief	Engineer, Construction, Facilities, and Equipment	Headquarters and service company in combat engineer and combat assault battalions; engineer company in combat assault battalion; engineer support company in combat engineer battalion	182	94.5	1.8
1361	Engineer Assistant	Engineer, Construction, Facilities, and Equipment	Headquarters and service company in combat engineer battalion	106	88.7	3.2
1371	Combat Engineer	Engineer, Construction, Facilities, and Equipment	Combat engineer company, headquarters and service company in combat engineer battalion; engineer company in combat assault battalion	3,017	56.0	2.8
2111	Small Arms Repairer/ Technician	Ground Ordnance Maintenance	Headquarters and service company in light armored reconnaissance, amphibious assault vehicle, reconnaissance, tank, infantry, combat engineer, and combat assault battalions; amphibious assault vehicle company in amphibious assault vehicle battalion; artillery battery in infantry battalion; combat assault company in infantry regiment; light armored reconnaissance company in light armored reconnaissance battalion; rocket battery in artillery battalion; tank company in tank battalion; headquarters battery in artillery battalion and low-altitude air defense battalion	1,318	72.3	3.5
2161	Machinist	Ground Ordnance Maintenance	Headquarters and service company in light armored reconnaissance, amphibious assault vehicle, tank, and combat assault battalions	131	85.5	1.2

Table B.7—Continued

Occupational Code	Title	Occupational/ Career Field	Location of Closed Positions	Total Authorizations	Percentage of Positions Open to Women	Percentage of Positions Filled by Women
2171	Electro-Optical Ordnance Repairer	Ground Ordnance Maintenance	Headquarters and service company in light armored reconnaissance, amphibious assault vehicle, reconnaissance, tank, infantry, and combat assault battalions; rocket battery in infantry regiment	514	55.3	1.4
2311	Ammunition Technician	Ammunition and Explosive Ordnance Disposal	Headquarters and service company in light armored reconnaissance, amphibious assault vehicle, reconnaissance, tank, infantry, combat engineer, and combat assault battalions; amphibious assault vehicle company in amphibious assault vehicle battalion; artillery battery in artillery battalion; rocket battery in artillery battalion; weapon company in infantry battalion; headquarters battery in artillery battalion	1,301	82.5	13.2
2821	Technical Controller Marine	Ground Electronics Maintenance	Company in infantry regiment	338	94.4	2.6
2844	Ground Communications Organizational Repairer	Ground Electronics Maintenance	Headquarters and service company in light armored reconnaissance, amphibious assault vehicle, reconnaissance, tank, infantry, combat engineer, and combat assault battalions; amphibious assault vehicle company in amphibious assault vehicle battalion; combat assault company in infantry regiment; light armored reconnaissance company in light armored reconnaissance battalion; tank company in tank battalion; headquarters battery in artillery battalion and low-altitude air defense battalion	979	54.5	2.2
2846	Ground Radio Intermediate Repairer	Ground Electronics Maintenance	Headquarters battery in low-altitude air defense battalion	549	99.6	3.1

Table B.7—Continued

Occupational Code	Title	Occupational/ Career Field	Location of Closed Positions	Total Authorizations	Percentage of Positions Open to Women	Percentage of Positions Filled by Women
2847	Telephone Systems/ Personal Computer Repairer	Ground Electronics Maintenance	Headquarters and service company in light armored reconnaissance, amphibious assault vehicle, reconnaissance, tank, infantry, combat engineer, and combat assault battalions; headquarters battery in artillery battalion and low-altitude air defense battalion	779	85.0	3.2
2862	Electronics Maintenance Technician	Ground Electronics Maintenance	Headquarters and service company in light armored reconnaissance, amphibious assault vehicle, reconnaissance, tank, infantry, and combat engineer battalions; amphibious assault vehicle company in amphibious assault vehicle battalion; headquarters battery in artillery battalion and low-altitude air defense battalion	651	86.2	3.6
2887	Artillery Electronics Technician	Ground Electronics Maintenance	Detachment headquarters battery in infantry battalion	76	94.7	0.0
2891	Electronics Maintenance Chief	Ground Electronics Maintenance	Headquarters and service company in amphibious assault vehicle, tank, and combat assault battalions; headquarters company in infantry regiment	122	86.1	0.0
3043	Supply Administration and Operations Specialist	Food Supply Administration and Operations	Headquarters and service company in light armored reconnaissance, amphibious assault vehicle, reconnaissance, tank, infantry, combat engineer, and combat assault battalions; amphibious assault vehicle company in amphibious assault vehicle battalion; artillery battery in artillery battalion; rocket battery in artillery battalion; headquarters battery in artillery battalion and low-altitude air defense battalion	3,635	85.6	19.6

Table B.7—Continued

Occupational Code	Title	Occupational/ Career Field	Location of Closed Positions	Total Authorizations	Percentage of Positions Open to Women	Percentage of Positions Filled by Women
3051	Warehouse Clerk	Food Supply Administration and Operations	Headquarters and service company in light armored reconnaissance, amphibious assault vehicle, reconnaissance, tank, infantry, combat engineer, and combat assault battalions; amphibious assault vehicle company in amphibious assault vehicle battalion; tank company in tank battalion; headquarters battery in artillery battalion and low-altitude air defense battalion	2,436	86.1	20.4
3052	Packaging Specialist	Food Supply Administration and Operations	Headquarters and service company in combat assault battalion	195	99.5	20.1
3381	Food Service Specialist	Food Service	Headquarters and service company in light armored reconnaissance, amphibious assault vehicle, tank, infantry, combat engineer, and combat assault battalions; headquarters battery in artillery battalion	2,091	77.2	14.6
3521	Automotive Maintenance Technician	Motor Transport	Headquarters and service company in light armored reconnaissance, amphibious assault vehicle, tank, infantry, and combat assault battalion; amphibious assault vehicle company in amphibious assault vehicle battalion; artillery battery in artillery battalion; engineer company in combat assault battalion; engineer support company in combat engineer battalion; rocket battery in artillery battalion; headquarters battery in artillery battalion and low-altitude air defense battalion	3,857	78.8	2.6

Table B.7—Continued

Occupational Code	Title	Occupational/ Career Field	Location of Closed Positions	Total Authorizations	Percentage of Positions Open to Women	Percentage of Positions Filled by Women
3529	Motor Transport Maintenance Chief	Motor Transport	Headquarters and service company in light armored reconnaissance, amphibious assault vehicle, tank, infantry, and combat assault battalions; engineer company in combat assault battalion; engineer support company in combat engineer battalion; headquarters battery in artillery battalion and low-altitude air defense battalion	677	86.6	2.6
3531	Motor Vehicle Operator	Motor Transport	Headquarters and service company in light armored reconnaissance, amphibious assault vehicle, tank, infantry, and combat assault battalions; amphibious assault vehicle company in amphibious assault vehicle battalion; artillery battery in artillery battalion; combat assault company in infantry regiment; engineer company in combat assault battalion; engineer support company in combat engineer battalion; rocket battery in artillery battalion; weapon company in infantry battalion; headquarters battery in artillery battalion and low-altitude air defense battalion	7,598	76.3	4.6
3537	Motor Transport Operations Chief	Motor Transport	Headquarters and service company in light armored reconnaissance, amphibious assault vehicle, tank, infantry, and combat assault battalions; amphibious assault vehicle company in amphibious assault vehicle battalion; artillery battery in artillery battalion; engineer company in combat assault battalion; engineer support company in combat engineer battalion; rocket battery in artillery battalion; headquarters battery in artillery battalion and low-altitude air defense battalion	866	81.9	4.0

Table B.7—Continued

Occupational Code	Title	Occupational/ Career Field	Location of Closed Positions	Total Authorizations	Percentage of Positions Open to Women	Percentage of Positions Filled by Women
4421	Legal Services Specialist	Legal Services	Headquarters and service company in amphibious assault vehicle battalion	474	99.8	23.4
4821	Career Retention Specialist	Recruiting and Retention	Headquarters and service company in light armored reconnaissance, amphibious assault vehicle, reconnaissance, tank, infantry, combat engineer, and combat assault battalions; headquarters battery in artillery battalion and low-altitude air defense battalion	376	83.8	16.5
5711	Marine Combat Instructor	Chemical, Biological, Radiological, and Nuclear Defense	Headquarters and service company in light armored reconnaissance, amphibious assault vehicle, reconnaissance, tank, infantry, combat engineer, and combat assault battalions; rocket battery in artillery battalion; headquarters battery in artillery battalion and low-altitude air defense battalion	786	79.3	6.3
8013 (FMOS)	Special Assignment—Enlisted	Miscellaneous Requirements	Headquarters company in infantry regiment	11	27.3	0.0
8014 (FMOS)	Billet Designator—Enlisted	Miscellaneous Requirements	Headquarters and service company in reconnaissance battalion; headquarters company in infantry regiment	475	90.3	7.9
8711 (EMOS)	Ground Operations Specialist	Miscellaneous Requirements	Headquarters and service company in combat assault battalion and when required PMOS is closed	121	97.5	5.0
8911 (FMOS)	Billet Designer—Barracks and Grounds Marine	Miscellaneous Requirements	Headquarters company in infantry regiment	132	93.9	6.8

Table B.7—Continued

Occupational Code	Title	Occupational/ Career Field	Location of Closed Positions	Total Authorizations	Percentage of Positions Open to Women	Percentage of Positions Filled by Women
8999	Sergeant Major–First Sergeant	Miscellaneous Requirements	Closed below the division level in ground combat element and low-altitude air defense battalion	1,218	72.9	5.2

SOURCES: Data on total authorizations are from TFSMS, January 2011. Marine Corps WISR representatives identified which positions are open to women. Data on the percentage of positions filled by women are from DEERS PITE personnel files, December 2010.

NOTE: All occupational codes are for PMOSs except where noted. A free MOS (FMOS) can be filled by any Marine regardless of PMOS; FMOSs are unrelated to PMOS skills. A billet is not restricted based on any particular FMOS. However, if that billet is located in a unit in which female assignments are restricted, then that billet will also be restricted. An exception MOS (EMOS) is generally the same as an FMOS, but it includes exceptions that require a specific PMOS or special skill. Closed positions listed in the table are located below the division level in the ground combat elements, except where otherwise noted.

Table B.8
Navy Officer and Warrant Officer Occupations with Some Positions Closed to Women

Billet Designator (Occupational Code)	Officer Title	Occupational/ Career Field	Location of Closed Positions	Total Authorizations	Percentage of Positions Open to Women	Percentage of Positions Filled by Women
111X	Unrestricted line officer who is qualified in surface warfare	Surface Warfare	NGLO to Marine Corps units below the division level in ground combat element, riverine boat officer positions	3,747	99.0	15.2
112X	Unrestricted line officer who is qualified in submarine warfare	Undersea Warfare	Fast-attack submarines	2,021	69.8	0.0
1170	Unrestricted line officer who is in training for submarine warfare qualification	Undersea Warfare	Fast-attack submarines	292	44.5	2.6
1300	Unrestricted line officer billet, Code 0—other than operational flying, requiring air warfare specialty of (or previous designation as) a pilot or naval flight officer	Aviation	NGLO positions	946	99.3	13.7
2100	Medical Corps Officer	Staff Corps	Marine Corps units below the division level in ground combat element	3,402	97.6	25.3 in 191X, 196X, and 197X (all in instruction); 210X, 270X (O7 rank); cannot break out 2100
310X	Supply Corps Officer	Staff Corps	Fast-attack submarines	2,109	97.3	13.6 in 310X and 316X (in training), cannot break out 310X

Table B.8—Continued

Billet Designator (Occupational Code)	Officer Title	Occupational/ Career Field	Location of Closed Positions	Total Authorizations	Percentage of Positions Open to Women	Percentage of Positions Filled by Women
4100	Chaplain Corps Officer	Staff Corps	Marine Corps units below the division level in ground combat element	899	92.2	7.3 in 194X (prospective chaplain) and 410X, cannot break out 4100
6120	Limited Duty Officer, Operations (Surface)	Surface Warfare	NGLO to Marine Corps units below the division level in ground combat element	222	95.0	1.3
6400	Limited Duty Officer, Nuclear Power	Undersea Warfare	Submarine-specific positions are closed (require prior enlisted experience on subs)	397	95.0	0.8
6510	Limited Duty Officer, Supply Corps	Staff Corps	Submarine-specific positions are closed (requires prior enlisted experience on subs)	130	92.3	17.5
7120	Warrant Officer, Operations Technician	Surface Warfare	NGLO to Marine Corps units below the division level in ground combat element	90	91.1	4.3

SOURCES: The locations of closed positions and percentage of positions open to women are derived from OPNAVINST 1300.17B (2011), discussions with Navy representatives, and June 2011 TFMMS data. June 2011 data on the percentage of positions filled provided by Navy WISR representatives.

Table B.9
Navy Enlisted Occupations with Some Positions Closed to Women

Rating	Title	Occupational Field	Location of Closed Positions	Total Authorizations	Percentage of Positions Open to Women	Percentage of Positions Filled by Women
BM	Boatswain's Mate	General Seamanship	Riverine squadrons, submarines, and frigates	5,018	91.5	17.1
CE	Construction Electrician	Construction	Riverine squadrons	1,139	99.7	14.7
CM	Construction Mechanic	Construction	Riverine squadrons	2,299	99.9	4.5
CS	Culinary Specialist	Logistics	Riverine boat teams, patrol craft, submarines, and frigates	7,333	88.1	18.9
CT	Cryptologic Technician	Cryptology	Special operations teams, frigates, and submarines	9,431	92.6	21.6
DC	Damage Control	Ship Maintenance	Riverine boat teams, patrol craft, and frigates	2,598	94.5	16.6
EM	Electrician	Marine Engineering	Riverine boat teams, patrol craft, and submarines	5,979	69.6	10.2
EN	Engineman	Marine Engineering	Riverine squadrons, patrol craft, and frigates	4,635	93.5	12.5
ET	Electronics Technician	Weapons Control	Frigates, patrol craft, riverine squadrons, submarines (including ETR Electronic Technician Radio and ETN Electronic Technician Navigator ratings)	11,029	57.9	9.7
FC	Fire Control	Weapons Control	Patrol craft and frigates	5,973	96.0	11.7
GM	Gunner's Mate	Ordnance Systems	Riverine squadrons and frigates	3,615	93.2	13.6
GS	Gas Turbine Systems	Marine Engineering	Frigates	3,743	89.3	13.1

Table B.9—Continued

Rating	Title	Occupational Field	Location of Closed Positions	Total Authorizations	Percentage of Positions Open to Women	Percentage of Positions Filled by Women
HM (includes HN)	Hospital Corpsman	Health Care	Riverine boat reams, patrol craft, submarines, frigates, and Marine Corps units below the division level in ground combat element	23,254	76.7	19.9
HT	Hull Maintenance	Ship Maintenance	Riverine squadrons, frigate, and patrol craft	2,234	96.3	11.6
IC	Interior Communications	Marine Engineering	Frigates	1,872	95.5	22.1
IS	Intelligence Specialist	Intelligence	Patrol craft and submarine-related NECs	2,689	99.9	23.6
IT	Information Systems (including ITS Information Systems Technician submarine rating)	Communications	Frigates, riverine boat teams, patrol craft, submarines	9,862	85.9	26.5
LS	Logistics Specialist	Logistics	Submarines, patrol craft, frigates	8,796	95.3	23.5
MA	Master-at-Arms	Law Enforcement/ Security	Riverine squadrons, submarines, and frigates	8,959	99.4	17.8
MM	Machinists Mate (including MME Machinists Mate Auxiliary and MMW Machinists Mate Weapons ratings)	Marine Engineering	Frigates, submarines, and riverine squadrons, submarines	12,598	54.1	8.2
MR	Machinery	Ship Maintenance	Frigates	565	95.6	13.2
NC	Navy Counselor	Administration	Riverine squadrons and frigates	1,429	98.2	24.4

Table B.9—Continued

Rating	Title	Occupational Field	Location of Closed Positions	Total Authorizations	Percentage of Positions Open to Women	Percentage of Positions Filled by Women
OS	Operations Specialist	Ship Operations	Riverine boat teams, patrol craft, submarines, and frigates	6,929	93.3	23.1
PS	Personnel Specialist	Administration	Patrol craft and frigates	2,382	98.1	27.7
QM	Quartermaster	Ship Operations	Riverine boat teams, frigates, patrol craft	1,987	87.5	22.8
RP	Religious Program	Administration	Riverine squadrons and Marine Corps units below the division level in ground combat element	747	59.0	26.2
SH	Ship Serviceman	Logistics	Frigates	1,982	94.8	22.7
SN	Seaman	General Seamanship	Frigates	4,014	87.8	18.4
STG	Sonar Technician Surface	Sensor Operations	Frigates and submarine-related NECs	2,587	78.4	15.4
YN	Yeoman	Administration	Submarines, patrol craft, and frigates	5,280	93.7	30.2

SOURCES: The locations of closed positions are derived from OPNAVINST 1300.17B (2011), discussions with Navy representatives, and June 2011 TFMMS data. Data on total authorizations are from TFMMS, June 2011. Data on the percentage of positions open to women are from TFMMS, June 2011; Navy policy; and Navy WISR and career field representatives in 2011. June 2011 data on the percentage of positions filled provided by the Navy.

APPENDIX C

Army and Marine Corps Positions by Career Field

Because the Army and Marine Corps tables in Appendixes A and B were particularly lengthy, this appendix provides a more succinct overview of the total number of authorizations, the percentage open to women, and percentage filled by women.

Table C.1
Army Authorized Positions, Percentage of Positions Open to Women, and Percentage of Positions Filled by Women, by Career Field

Occupational Field	Total Authorizations	Percentage of Positions Open to Women	Percentage of Positions Filled by Women
11 Infantry	61,594	0	0
12 (21 in 2004–2008) Corps of Engineers	22,212	50	5
13 Field Artillery	26,948	7	0
14 Air Defense Artillery	8,009	98	10
15 Aviation	26,894	91	7
18 Special Forces	7,482	0	0
19 Armor	19,736	0	0
24 Telecommunications System Engineering	255	100	7
25 Signal Corps/ Communications and Information Systems Operation	33,256	85	14
27 Judge Advocate General Corps/Paralegal	3,242	92	31
29 Electronic Warfare	382	57	7
30 Information Operations	379	99.7	6
31 Military Police	19,030	99.8	14
34 Strategic Intelligence	265	100	9
35 Military Intelligence	24,993	88	18
36 Financial Management	2,215	99	32

Table C.1—Continued

Occupational Field	Total Authorizations	Percentage of Positions Open to Women	Percentage of Positions Filled by Women
37 Psychological Operations	1,387	83	12
38 Civil Affairs	1,046	92	10
40 Space Operations	247	100	6
42 Adjutant General Corps	16,181	87	40
46 Public Affairs	1,244	99.8	30
47 United States Military Academy Stabilized Faculty	113	100	15
48 Foreign Area Officer	888	100	6
49 Operations Research/ Systems Analysis	444	100	7
50 Force Management	207	99.5	9
51 Research, Development and Acquisition/ Acquisition, Logistics and Technology	1,990	99	14
52 Nuclear and Counterproliferation	212	100	6
53 Systems Automation Officer	665	99	12
56 Chaplain/Religious Support	3,025	84	15
57 Simulations Operations	263	99	5
59 Strategist	333	99.6	8
60 Medical Corps (officers only)	1,735	99.9	29
61 Medical Corps (officers only)	2,046	98	20
62 Medical Corps (officers only)	381	92	18
63 Dental Corps (officers only)	956	100	17
64 Veterinary Corps (officers only)	515	100	47
65 Army Medical Specialists Corps (officers only)	1,195	80	34
66 Army Nurse Corps (officers only)	3,158	100	64
67 Medical Service Corps (officers only)	842	100	28
68 Medical (all enlisted medical)	30,395	78	28
70 Health Services (officers only)	2,096	90	28
71 Laboratory Sciences (officers only)	235	100	25
72 Preventive Medicine Sciences (officers only)	418	100	32

Table C.1—Continued

Occupational Field	Total Authorizations	Percentage of Positions Open to Women	Percentage of Positions Filled by Women
73 Behavioral Sciences (officers only)	258	99	46
74 Chemical, Biological, Radiological, Nuclear (CBRN)	8,038	80	23
79 Recruitment and Reenlistment (enlisted only)	4,033	99.9	11
88 Transportation	23,050	99	16
89 Ammunition	5,507	98	14
90 Logistics	2,697	97	18
91 Ordnance/Mechanical Maintenance	37,702	88	7
92 Quartermaster Corps/Supply and Services	49,764	90	29
94 Electronic Maintenance and Calibrations	4,785	95	8

SOURCE: Total authorization data from PMAD, March 2011. This column excludes a small number of miscellaneous positions that do not fall into these categories. Data on the percentage of positions open to women are from PMAD, March 2011. Some entries are not rounded to avoid implying a full 100 percent. Data on the percentage of positions filled by women are from DEERS PITE personnel files, December 2010.

NOTE: Where the officer and enlisted field titles differ, the officer title is presented first, followed by the enlisted title. Data on total authorizations exclude authorizations in miscellaneous MOSs that do not fall into career fields.

Table C.2
Marine Corps Authorized Positions, Percentage of Positions Open to Women, and Percentage of Positions Filled by Women, by Career Field

Occupational Field	Total Authorizations	Percentage of Positions Open to Women	Percentage of Positions Filled by Women
01 Personnel and Administration	7,180	94	23
02 Intelligence	3,983	85	10
03 Infantry	28,520	0	0
04 Logistics	4,867	86	12
05 Marine Air Ground Task Force (MAGTF) Plans	649	95	8
06 Communications	14,007	68	8
08 Field Artillery	4,669	0	0
09 Training	2,285	100	5
11 Utilities	2,538	91	8
13 Engineer, Construction, Facilities, and Equipment	8,023	77	3
18 Tank and Assault Amphibious Vehicle	2,886	0	0
21 Ground Ordnance Maintenance	3,977	37	2
23 Ammunition and Explosive Ordnance Disposal	2,052	89	9
26 Signals Intelligence/Ground Electronic Warfare	2,264	100	12
27 Linguist	3	100	17
28 Ground Electronics Maintenance	4,193	83	3
30 Supply Administration and Operations	6,914	86	20
31 Distribution Management	549	100	19
33 Food Service	2,133	78	15
34 Financial Management	1,409	100	17
35 Motor Transport	13,104	78	4
41 Marine Corps Community Services	140	100	10
43 Public Affairs	495	100	25
44 Legal Services	854	99.9	17
46 Combat Camera	408	100	20
48 Recruiting and Retention	443	86	15

Table C.2—Continued

Occupational Field	Total Authorizations	Percentage of Positions Open to Women	Percentage of Positions Filled by Women
55 Music	884	100	17
57 Chemical, Biological, Radiological and Nuclear (CBRN) Defense	909	76	6
58 Military Police, Investigations, and Corrections	4,221	100	7
59 Electronics Maintenance	1,289	100	5
60 Aircraft Maintenance	4,730	100	8
63 Organizational Avionics Maintenance	3,564	100	8
65 Aviation Ordnance	2,458	100	6
66 Aviation Logistics	2,078	100	17
68 Meteorology and Oceanography (METOC)	355	100	8
70 Airfield Services	2,076	99.8	9
72 Air Control/Air Support/Antiair Warfare/Air	2,367	83	6
73 Navigation Office/Enlisted Flight Crews	171	100	4
75 Pilots/Naval Flight Officers	3,899	97	3

SOURCES: Data on total authorizations are from TFSMS, January 2011. Marine Corps WISR representatives identified which positions are open to women. Data on the percentage of positions filled by women are from DEERS PITE personnel files, December 2010.

NOTE: Data on total authorizations exclude authorizations in miscellaneous MOSs that do not fall into career fields.

APPENDIX D

Naval Vessel Limitations for Women

All enlisted positions on missile-guided frigates, patrol craft, and submarines are closed to women due to the costs of providing appropriate berthing and privacy arrangements. Female officers are prohibited from serving on fast-attack submarines. According to 2011 authorization data provided by the Navy, this translates to 4,040 positions on frigates, 424 positions on patrol craft, and 13,000 positions on submarines closed to female Sailors. The 369 positions on riverine boat crews (351 enlisted and 18 officers) are closed to women because of the direct ground combat missions of those crews, not because of berthing issues.

Table D.1 illustrates the variability of the degree of availability of enlisted berthing available to women on the types of ships that are open to them. The information is derived from July 2011 ship space data supplied by the Navy. According to December 2010 DEERS PITE data, 8 percent of Navy chief petty officers (pay grades E7–E9) are women, and 16 percent of enlisted women are at pay grades E3–E6.

Table D.1
Percentage of Enlisted Berthing Designated for Female Sailors on Navy Ships Open to Women

Ship	Number of Chief Petty Officer (E7–E9) Racks	Percentage of Chief Petty Officer Racks Available to Women	Number of Remaining Enlisted (E3–E6) Racks	Percentage of Remaining Enlisted Racks Available to Women
Submarine Tenders				
AS-39 *Emory S. Land*	19	47	111	19
AS-40 *Frank Cable*	141	11	753	16
Guided Missile Cruisers				
CG-52 *Bunker Hill*	33	18	345	10
CG-53 *Mobile Bay*	33	18	321	10
CG-54 *Antietam*	39	0	328	0
CG-55 *Leyte Gulf*	33	18	330	17
CG-56 *San Jacinto*	33	18	327	10
CG-57 *Lake Champlain*	32	0	319	0
CG-58 *Philippine Sea*	33	18	334	10
CG-59 *Princeton*	45	13	327	11
CG-60 *Normandy*	33	18	327	10
CG-61 *Monterey*	44	14	308	11
CG-62 *Chancellorsville*	33	9	336	11
CG-63 *Cowpens*	31	13	339	12
CG-64 *Gettysburg*	45	13	324	11
CG-65 *Chosin*	33	18	342	11
CG-66 *Hue City*	33	18	321	12
CG-67 *Shiloh*	30	10	286	9
CG-68 *Anzio*	33	0	321	0
CG-69 *Vicksburg*	45	0	339	0
CG-70 *Lake Erie*	33	0	327	0
CG-71 *Cape St. George*	44	0	321	0
CG-72 *Vella Gulf*	30	20	324	12
CG-73 *Port Royal*	33	18	335	12

Table D.1—Continued

Ship	Number of Chief Petty Officer (E7–E9) Racks	Percentage of Chief Petty Officer Racks Available to Women	Number of Remaining Enlisted (E3–E6) Racks	Percentage of Remaining Enlisted Racks Available to Women
Aircraft Carriers				
CVN-65 *Enterprise*	229	8	3,327	12
CVN-68 *Nimitz*	180	10	3,158	21
CVN-69 *Dwight D. Eisenhower*	276	15	3,481	16
CVN-70 *Carl Vinson*	248	6	3,458	11
CVN-71 *Theodore Roosevelt*	261	9	3,523	19
CVN-72 *Abraham Lincoln*	234	10	3,293	19
CVN-73 *George Washington*	195	9	3,231	15
CVN-74 *John C. Stennis*	213	8	3,838	13
CVN-75 *Harry S. Truman*	203	15	3,224	19
CVN-76 *Ronald Reagan*	174	8	3,924	26
CVN-77 *George H. W. Bush*	227	12	3,400	18
Guided Missile Destroyers				
DDG-51 *Arleigh Burke*	28	21	246	24
DDG-52 *Barry*	27	11	291	14
DDG-53 *John Paul Jones*	24	13	300	28
DDG-54 *Curtis Wilbur*	27	11	294	13
DDG-55 *Stout*	27	11	291	21
DDG-56 *John S. McCain*	24	0	297	0
DDG-57 *Mitscher*	27	0	300	0
DDG-58 *Laboon*	27	11	291	21
DDG-59 *Russell*	27	0	291	0
DDG-60 *Paul Hamilton*	27	22	273	22
DDG-61 *Ramage*	24	0	297	0
DDG-62 *Fitzgerald*	27	11	291	14
DDG-63 *Stethem*	27	11	291	8
DDG-64 *Carney*	27	11	273	15
DDG-65 *Benfold*	27	11	277	28

Table D.1—Continued

Ship	Number of Chief Petty Officer (E7–E9) Racks	Percentage of Chief Petty Officer Racks Available to Women	Number of Remaining Enlisted (E3–E6) Racks	Percentage of Remaining Enlisted Racks Available to Women
DDG-66 *Gonzalez*	27	11	291	21
DDG-67 *Cole*	27	11	324	19
DDG-68 *The Sullivans*	27	11	297	20
DDG-69 *Milius*	27	11	295	12
DDG-70 *Hopper*	45	7	281	21
DDG-71 *Ross*	27	22	273	22
DDG-72 *Mahan*	27	11	291	15
DDG-73 *Decatur*	27	11	303	14
DDG-74 *McFaul*	27	22	288	15
DDG-75 *Donald Cook*	36	17	282	15
DDG-76 *Higgins*	24	13	303	14
DDG-77 *O'Kane*	30	10	293	20
DDG-78 *Porter*	27	11	300	22
DDG-79 *Oscar Austin*	27	11	306	22
DDG-80 *Roosevelt*	27	11	306	22
DDG-81 *Winston S. Churchill*	27	22	257	26
DDG-82 *Lassen*	27	11	324	20
DDG-83 *Howard*	27	11	324	21
DDG-84 *Bulkeley*	27	22	323	23
DDG-85 *McCampbell*	30	20	300	20
DDG-86 *Shoup*	27	11	302	19
DDG-87 *Mason*	45	7	306	22
DDG-88 *Preble*	24	17	244	26
DDG-89 *Mustin*	27	11	324	14
DDG-90 *Chafee*	27	11	322	20
DDG-91 *Pinckney*	26	12	294	23
DDG-92 *Momsen*	27	11	282	17
DDG-93 *Chung-Hoon*	27	22	312	15

Table D.1—Continued

Ship	Number of Chief Petty Officer (E7–E9) Racks	Percentage of Chief Petty Officer Racks Available to Women	Number of Remaining Enlisted (E3–E6) Racks	Percentage of Remaining Enlisted Racks Available to Women
DDG-94 *Nitze*	27	22	312	21
DDG-95 *James E. Williams*	27	11	273	24
DDG-96 *Bainbridge*	27	22	312	21
DDG-97 *Halsey*	27	11	312	15
DDG-98 *Forrest Sherman*	27	11	304	22
DDG-99 *Farragut*	27	11	258	9
DDG-100 *Kidd*	26	12	239	23
DDG-101 *Gridley*	26	12	239	23
DDG-102 *Sampson*	45	13	276	17
DDG-103 *Truxtun*	27	22	237	20
DDG-104 *Sterett*	26	12	232	21
DDG-105 *Dewey*	26	12	239	23
DDG-106 *Stockdale*	27	11	255	15
DDG-107 *Gravely*	26	12	239	23
DDG-108 *Wayne E. Meyer*	26	12	239	23
DDG-109 *Jason Dunham*	27	11	255	19
DDG-110 *William P. Lawrence*	26	12	239	23
DDG-111 *Spruance*	26	12	239	23
Command Ship				
LCC-19 *Blue Ridge*	66	14	1,125	9
Amphibious Assault Ships				
LHA-5 *Peleliu*	83	11	1,001	11
LHD-1 *Wasp*	82	11	1,116	19
LHD-2 *Essex*	85	11	1,114	16
LHD-3 *Kearsarge*	83	11	1,110	19
LHD-4 *Boxer*	105	9	1,057	16
LHD-5 *Bataan*	77	12	1,011	21
LHD-6 *Bonhomme Richard*	76	11	1,061	20

Table D.1—Continued

Ship	Number of Chief Petty Officer (E7–E9) Racks	Percentage of Chief Petty Officer Racks Available to Women	Number of Remaining Enlisted (E3–E6) Racks	Percentage of Remaining Enlisted Racks Available to Women
LHD-7 *Iwo Jima*	87	10	1,068	20
LHD-8 *Makin Island*	78	12	1,110	19
Amphibious Transport Docks				
LPD-9 *Denver*	28	0	462	0
LPD-15 *Ponce*	28	0	356	0
LPD-17 *San Antonio*	45	13	397	15
LPD-18 *New Orleans*	45	13	330	23
LPD-19 *Mesa Verde*	32	13	331	24
LPD-20 *Green Bay*	28	21	330	22
LPD-21 *New York*	45	13	397	15
LPD-22 *San Diego*	45	13	397	15
Landing Craft Carriers				
LSD-41 *Whidbey Island*	29	17	411	21
LSD-42 *Germantown*	42	7	360	25
LSD-43 *Fort McHenry*	26	8	411	14
LSD-44 *Gunston Hall*	31	19	360	25
LSD-45 *Comstock*	22	9	372	27
LSD-46 *Tortuga*	24	8	417	14
LSD-47 *Rushmore*	29	17	345	34
LSD-48 *Ashland*	26	15	340	21
LSD-49 *Harpers Ferry*	24	8	363	25
LSD-50 *Carter Hall*	28	7	429	13
LSD-51 *Oak Hill*	33	18	345	22
LSD-52 *Pearl Harbor*	27	11	355	43

SOURCE: Ship space data supplied by Navy WISR representatives.

Bibliography

Air Force Instruction 36-2110, *Personnel Assignments*, Washington, D.C.: U.S. Department of the Air Force, September 22, 2009.

Air Force Special Operations Command, "Tactical Air Control Party," web page, undated. As of May 31, 2011:
http://www.afsoc.af.mil/specialtactics/tacp

American Bureau of Shipping, *Naval and Government Vessels: Classification and Certification Services*, Houston, Tex., January 1, 2008. As of August 25, 2011:
http://www.eagle.org/eagleExternalPortalWEB/ShowProperty/BEA%20Repository/References/Capability%20Brochures/NavalCp

Army Regulation 600-13, *Army Policy for the Assignment of Female Soldiers*, Washington, D.C.: Headquarters, U.S. Department of the Army, March 27, 1992.

Asch, Beth J., Trey Miller, and Alessandro Malchiodi, *A New Look at Gender and Minority Officer Career Progression in the Military*, Santa Monica, Calif.: RAND Corporation, forthcoming.

Aspin, Les, Secretary of Defense, "Direct Combat Definition and Assignment Rule," memorandum, January 13, 1994.

Baldor, Lolita, "Women Breaking Barriers in Navy, Not SEALs Yet," Associated Press, May 30, 2011.

Beckett, Megan K., and Chiaying Sandy Chien, *The Status of Gender Integration in the Military: Supporting Appendices*, Santa Monica, Calif.: RAND Corporation, MR-1381-OSD, 2002. As of August 12, 2011:
http://www.rand.org/pubs/monograph_reports/MR1381.html

Binkin, Martin, *Who Will Fight the Next War? The Changing Face of the American Military*, Washington, D.C.: Brookings Institution Press, 1993.

Binkin, Martin, and Shirley J. Bach, *Women and the Military*, Washington, D.C.: Brookings Institution Press, 1977.

Bumiller, Elisabeth, "For Female Marines, Tea Comes with Bullets," *New York Times*, October 2, 2010. As of August 29, 2011:
http://www.nytimes.com/2010/10/03/world/asia/03marines.html

Cawkill, Paul, Alison Rogers, Sarah Knight, and Laura Spear, *Women in Ground Close Combat Roles: The Experiences of Other Nations and a Review of the Academic Literature*, Fareham, Hampshire, UK: Defense Science and Technology Laboratory, DSTL/CR37770 V3-0, September 29, 2009.

Clare, Micah E., "2nd Woman Since WWII Gets Silver Star," Army News Service, March 21, 2008. As of August 28, 2011:
http://www.army.mil/article/8068

COMNAVAIRPAC Instruction 1300.2A/COMNAVSURFPAC Instruction 1300.2, *Embarkation of Women at Sea*, San Diego, Calif.: Commander, Naval Air Force, U.S. Pacific Fleet, and Commander, Naval Surface Force, U.S. Pacific Fleet, June 22, 2000.

Conley, Raymond E., and Albert A. Robbert, *Air Force Officer Specialty Structure: Reviewing the Fundamentals*, Santa Monica, Calif.: RAND Corporation, TR-637-AF, 2009. As of August 26, 2011: http://www.rand.org/pubs/technical_reports/TR637.html

DACOWITS—*see* Defense Advisory Committee on Women in the Services.

Dalton, John H., Secretary of the Navy, "Direct Ground Combat Definition and Assignment Rule," memorandum, April 29, 1994.

Davis, K. D., and Virginia Thomas, *Gender Integration Study: The Experience of Women Who Have Served in the Combat Arms*, Ottawa, Ontario: National Defence Headquarters, January 1998.

Defense Advisory Committee on Women in the Services, *Defense Advisory Committee on Women in the Services 2009 Report*, Washington, D.C., March 23, 2010. As of August 25, 2011: http://dacowits.defense.gov/Reports/2009/Annual%20Report/dacowits2009report.pdf

Defense Manpower Data Center, "Military Casualty Information," web page, data as of October 3, 2011. As of October 26, 2011: http://siadapp.dmdc.osd.mil/personnel/CASUALTY/castop.htm

DMDC—*see* Defense Manpower Data Center.

Dorn, Edwin, "Under Secretary of Defense (Personnel and Readiness), Application of the Direct Ground Combat Definition and Assignment Rule," memorandum, July 28, 1994.

Ebbert, Jean, and Marie-Beth Hall, *Crossed Currents: Navy Women in a Century of Change*, 3rd ed., Washington, D.C.: Batsford Brassey, 1999.

Ellery, David, "Battle Ahead for ADF Women," *Canberra Times*, September 28, 2011.

Feickert, Andrew, *U.S. Special Operations Forces (SOF): Background and Issues for Congress*, Washington, D.C.: Congressional Research Service, RS21048, July 15, 2011.

Fogarty, G. P., *Defence Instructions (Army): Army Physical Conditioning Assessment System*, Canberra, Australia: Australian Army, October 13, 2009.

GAO—*see* U.S. General Accounting Office.

Gates, Robert, Secretary of Defense, letter regarding changes to U.S. Navy policy on the assignment of women to submarines, to Vice President Joseph R. Biden, Jr., Representative Nancy Pelosi, Senator Carl Levin, and Representative Ike Skelton, Washington, D.C., February, 19, 2010.

Godson, Susan H., *Serving Proudly: A History of Women in the U.S. Navy*, Annapolis, Md.: U.S. Naval Institute Press, 2002.

Hamilton, John K., "Navy's First Riverine Squadron Deploys," Navy News Service, March 8, 2007. As of September 10, 2011: http://www.navy.mil/search/display.asp?story_id=28208

Harrell, Margaret C., Megan K. Beckett, Chiaying Sandy Chien, and Jerry M. Sollinger, *The Status of Gender Integration in the Military: Analysis of Selected Occupations*, Santa Monica, Calif.: RAND Corporation, MR-1380-OSD, 2002. As of August 12, 2011: http://www.rand.org/pubs/monograph_reports/MR1380.html

Harrell, Margaret C., Laura Werber Castaneda, Peter Schirmer, Bryan W. Hallmark, Jennifer Kavanagh, Daniel Gershwin, and Paul Steinberg, *Assessing the Assignment Policy for Army Women*, Santa Monica, Calif.: RAND Corporation, MG-590-1-OSD, 2007. As of August 12, 2011: http://www.rand.org/pubs/monographs/MG590-1.html

Harrell, Margaret C., and Laura. L. Miller, *New Opportunities for Military Women: Effects upon Readiness, Cohesion, and Morale*, Santa Monica, Calif.: RAND Corporation, MR-896-OSD, 1997. As of August 12, 2011:
http://www.rand.org/pubs/monograph_reports/MR896.html

Headquarters U.S. Air Force Personnel Center, *Air Force Enlisted Classification Directory (AFECD): The Official Guide to the Air Force Enlisted Classification Codes*, Washington, D.C., April 30, 2011a.

———, *Air Force Officer Classification Directory (AFOCD): The Official Guide to the Air Force Officer Classification Codes*, Washington, D.C., April 30, 2011b.

Headquarters, U.S. Department of the Army, *Military Occupational Classification and Structure*, Department of the Army Pamphlet 611-21, Washington, D.C., 2007.

———, *Multiple Launch Rocket System (MLRS) Operations*, Field Manual 3-09.60, Washington, D.C., August 12, 2008.

———, *Commissioned Officer Professional Development and Career Management*, Department of the Army Pamphlet 600-3, Washington, D.C., February 1, 2010.

Holm, Jeanne, *Women in the Military: An Unfinished Revolution*, rev. ed., Novato, Calif.: Presidio Press, 1993.

Hosek, Susan D., Peter Tiemeyer, M. Rebecca Kilburn, Debra A. Strong, Selika Ducksworth, and Reginald Ray, *Minority and Gender Differences in Officer Career Progression*, Santa Monica, Calif.: RAND Corporation, MR-1184-OSD, 2001. As of August 12, 2011:
http://www.rand.org/pubs/monograph_reports/MR1184.html

HQDA—*see* Headquarters, U.S. Department of the Army.

Iskra, Darlene M. "Attitudes Toward Expanding Roles for Navy Women at Sea: Results of a Content Analysis," *Armed Forces & Society*, Vol. 33, No. 2, January 2007, pp. 203–223.

Johnston, R. B., Deputy Chief of Staff for Manpower and Reserve Affairs, Headquarters, U.S. Marine Corps, "Review of Units and Positions (Military Occupational Specialties) Relative to the DoD Direct Ground Combat Definition and Assignment Rule," memorandum, April 19, 1994.

Kirby, Sheila Nataraj, Margaret C. Harrell, and Jennifer Sloan, "Why Don't Minorities Join Special Operations Forces?" *Armed Forces & Society*, Vol. 26, No. 4, Summer 2000, pp. 523–545.

Lim, Nelson, Jefferson P. Marquis, Kimberly Curry Hall, David Schulker, and Xiaohui Zhou, *Officer Classification and the Future of Diversity Among Senior Military Leaders: A Case Study of the Army ROTC*, Santa Monica, Calif.: RAND Corporation, TR-731-OSD, 2009. As of August 28, 2011:
http://www.rand.org/pubs/technical_reports/TR731.html

Lioness, dir. Meg McLagan and Daria Sommers, Room 11 Productions, 2008.

Manacapilli, Thomas, and Steven Buhrow, *Feasibility of an Air Liaison Officer Career Field: Improving the Theater Air-Ground System*, Santa Monica, Calif.: RAND Corporation, MG-755-AF, 2008. As of August 12, 2011:
http://www.rand.org/pubs/monographs/MG755.html

Manning, Lory, *Women in the Military: Where They Stand*, 7th ed., Washington, D.C.: Women's Research and Education Institute, November 2010.

Marine Corps Administrative Message 026/11, "Advance Notice of Forthcoming Changes to MCO P1300.8R Marine Corps Personnel Policy," January 13, 2011. As of August 27, 2011: http://www.marines.mil/news/messages/Pages/MARADMIN026-11.aspx

Marine Corps Order 1200.17A, *Military Occupational Specialties (MOS) Marine Corps Manual (Short Title: MOS Manual)*, Washington, D.C.: Headquarters, U.S. Marine Corps, June 4, 2009.

Marine Corps Order P1300.8R, *Marine Corps Personnel Assignment Policy*, Washington, D.C.: Headquarters, U.S. Marine Corps, October 4, 1994.

McHugh, John M., Secretary of the Army, "Fiscal Year 2011 (FY11) National Defense Authorization Act (NDAA) Review and Army Intent to Align Policy for the Assignment of Female Soldiers," memorandum to the Under Secretary of Defense for Personnel and Readiness, April 19, 2011.

Military Leadership Diversity Commission, *From Representation to Inclusion: Diversity Leadership for the 21st-Century Military*, Arlington, Va., March 15, 2011. As of September 29, 2011: http://mldc.whs.mil/index.php/final-report

Mitchell, Brian, *Women in the Military: Flirting with Disaster*, Washington, D.C., Regnery Publishing, 1998.

MLDC—*see* Military Leadership Diversity Commission.

Moore, Brenda L., *To Serve My Country, to Serve My Race: The Story of the Only African American WACs Stationed Overseas During World War II*, New York: New York University Press, 1996.

Moskos, Charles C., "Army Women," *Atlantic Magazine*, August 1990, pp. 70–78.

Naval Research Advisory Committee, *Quality of Life: Renewing Commitment to Our People*, Arlington, Va.: Office of the Assistant Secretary of the Navy for Research Development and Acquisition, March 2001.

Nishikawa, Brett R., Paul A. Sjoberg, and M. Maupin, *Medical Attrition of Battlefield Airmen Trainees*, Brooks City-Base, Tex.: Air Force Research Laboratory, AFRL-SA-BR-TR-2010-009, August 2010.

OPNAV Instruction 1300.17B, *Assignment of Women in the Navy*, Washington, D.C.: U.S. Department of the Navy, May 27, 2011.

OPNAV Instruction 1414.4B, *Navy Enlisted Fleet Marine Force Warfare Specialist Program*, Washington, D.C.: U.S. Department of the Navy, May 8, 2007.

OPNAV Instruction 6000.1C, *Navy Guidelines Concerning Pregnancy and Parenthood*, Washington, D.C.: U.S. Department of the Navy, June 14, 2007.

OPNAV Instruction 9640.1A, *Shipboard Habitability Program*, Washington, D.C.: U.S. Department of the Navy, September 3, 1996.

Perry, William J., Secretary of Defense, letter regarding changes in combat assignments for female members of the armed services, to Senator Sam Nunn and Representative Ronald V. Dellums, Washington, D.C., February 4, 1994.

———, letter regarding actions taken to expand the role of women in the military, to Representative Ronald V. Dellums, Washington, D.C., July 28, 1994.

Poulos, Paula Nassen, ed., *A Woman's War Too: U.S. Women in the Military in World War II*, Washington, D.C.: National Archives and Records Administration, 1996.

Presidential Commission on the Assignment of Women in the Armed Forces, *Women in Combat: Report to President*, Washington, D.C.: U.S. Government Printing Office, November 15, 1992.

Public Law 111-383, National Defense Authorization Act for Fiscal Year 2011, January 7, 2011.

Putko, Michele M., and Douglas V. Johnson II, eds., *Women in Combat Compendium*, Carlisle, Pa.: Strategic Studies Institute, U.S. Army War College, January 2008.

Robson, Seth, "A Woman's Touch: Engagement Teams Make Inroads with Afghanistan's Female Community," *Stars and Stripes*, October 9, 2010.

Rogan, Helen, *Mixed Company: Women in the Modern Army*, Boston, Mass.: Beacon Press, 1981.

Rostker, Bernard, *I Want You! The Evolution of the All-Volunteer Force*, Santa Monica, Calif.: RAND Corporation, MG-265-RC, 2006. As of August 28, 2011:
http://www.rand.org/pubs/monographs/MG265.html

Schneider, Dorothy, and Carl J. Schneider, *Sound Off! American Military Women Speak Out*, New York: Paragon House Publishers, 1992.

Secretary of the Navy Instruction 1300.12C, *Assignment of Women in the Department of the Navy*, Washington, D.C.: U.S. Department of the Navy, December 28, 2005.

Secretary of the Navy Instruction 1300.12C CH-1, *Assignment of Women in the Department of the Navy: Change Transmittal 1*, Washington, D.C.: U.S. Department of the Navy, May 14, 2009.

Segal, Mady Wechsler, "Women's Military Roles Cross-Nationally: Past, Present, and Future," *Gender and Society*, Vol. 9, No. 6, December 1995, pp. 757–775.

Simon, Rita James, ed., *Women in the Military*, New Brunswick, N.J.: Transaction Publishers, 2001.

Skaine, Rosemarie, *Women at War: Gender Issues of Americans in Combat*, Jefferson, N.C.: McFarland and Company, 1999

Soderbergh, Peter A., *Women Marines in the Korean War Era*, Westport, Conn.: Praeger Publishers, 1994.

Soucy, Jon, "Women's Museum Exhibit Features GWOT Silver Star Recipients," U.S. Army, October 27, 2008. As of August 28, 2011:
http://www.army.mil/article/13656

Stewart, Joshua, "SECNAV: Women Will Serve on Attack Subs," *Navy Times*, April 27, 2011. As of May 31, 2011:
http://www.navytimes.com/news/2011/04/navy-mabus-women-attack-submarines-042711w

Stiehm, Judith Hicks, *Bring Me Men and Women: Mandated Change at the U.S. Air Force Academy*, Berkeley and Los Angeles, Calif.: University of California Press, 1981.

———, *Arms and the Enlisted Woman*, Philadelphia, Pa.: Temple University Press, 1989.

Strauss, Gary, "'Lioness' Documentary Hunts Down Women's Role in Iraq War," *USA Today*, November 14, 2008. As of August 29, 2011:
http://www.usatoday.com/life/television/news/2008-11-12-lioness_N.htm

Talton, Trista, "MarSOC Looks to Women for New Mission," *Marine Corps Times*, November 14, 2009. As of August 29, 2011:
http://www.marinecorpstimes.com/news/2009/11/marines_marsoc_111409w

"Two Members of Cultural Support Team Receive Combat Action Badges," U.S. Army Special Operations Command, September 12, 2011. As of October 13, 2011:
http://www.soc.mil/UNS/Releases/2011/September/110912-06.htm

UK Ministry of Defence, Directorate of Service Personnel Policy Service Conditions, *Women in the Armed Forces*, London, May 2002. As of August 12, 2011:
http://www.mod.uk/NR/rdonlyres/10B34976-75F9-47E0-B376-AED4B09FB3B3/0/women_af_summary.pdf

U.S. Army John F. Kennedy Special Warfare Center and School, "About the Cultural Support Program," web page, undated. As of August 29, 2011:
http://www.soc.mil/SWCS/CST/about.html

U.S. Code, Title 10, Section 652, Notice to Congress of Proposed Changes in Units, Assignments, Etc. to Which Female Members May Be Assigned.

U.S. Department of the Navy, Bureau of Naval Personnel, *Naval Military Personnel Manual*, NAVPERS 15560D, Millington, Tenn., August 2002.

———, *Manual of Navy Enlisted Manpower and Personnel Classifications and Occupational Standards,* Vol. I: *Navy Enlisted Classifications (NECs),* NAVPERS 18068F, Washington, D.C., April 2011a.

———, *Manual of Navy Enlisted Manpower and Personnel Classifications and Occupational Standards,* Vol. II: *Navy Enlisted Classifications (NECs),* NAVPERS 18068F, Washington, D.C., July 2011b.

———, *Manual of Navy Officer Manpower and Personnel Classifications,* Vol. I: *Major Code Structures,* NAVPERS 15839I, Washington, D.C., July 2011c.

———, *Manual of Navy Officer Manpower and Personnel Classifications,* Vol. II: *The Officer Data Card,* NAVPERS 15839I, Washington, D.C., July 2011d.

U.S. General Accounting Office, *Women in the Military: Deployment in the Persian Gulf War,* Washington, D.C., GAO/NSIAD-93-93, July 1993. As of September 27, 2011:
http://archive.gao.gov/t2pbat5/149552.pdf

———, *Gender Issues: Analysis of Promotion and Career Opportunities Data*, Washington, D.C., GAO/NSIAD-98-157, May 1998a. As of September 27, 2011:
http://www.gao.gov/archive/1998/ns98157.pdf

———, *Gender Issues: Information on DoD's Assignment Policy and Direct Ground Combat Definition*, Washington, D.C., GAO/NSIAD-99-7, October 1998b. As of August 12, 2011:
http://www.gao.gov/archive/1999/ns99007.pdf

———, *Gender Issues: Perceptions of Readiness in Selected Units*, Washington, D.C., GAO/NSIAD-99-120, May 1999a. As of August 12, 2011:
http://www.gao.gov/archive/1999/ns99120.pdf

———, *Gender Issues: Trends in the Occupational Distribution of Military Women*, Washington, D.C., GAO/NSIAD-99-212, September 1999b. As of August 12, 2011:
http://www.gao.gov/archive/1999/ns99212.pdf

West, Togo D., Jr., Secretary of the Army, "Increasing Opportunities for Women in the Army," memorandum, July 27, 1994.

Widnall, Sheila E., Secretary of the Air Force, "Direct Ground Combat Definition and Assignment Rule (SECDEF Memo, 13 January 1994)," memorandum, June 21, 1994.

Zlatoper, R. J., U.S. Department of the Navy, Bureau of Naval Personnel, "Review of Units and Positions Relative to the DoD Direct Ground Combat Definition and Assignment Rule," memorandum, April 1994.